The Secret L

NOREEN MACKEY

The Secret
Ladder

DARTON · LONGMAN + TODD

First published in 2005 by
Darton, Longman and Todd Ltd
1 Spencer Court
140–142 Wandsworth High Street
London SW18 4JJ

ISBN 0 232 52595 1

A catalogue record for this book is available from the British Library.

Designed and produced by Sandie Boccacci
using QuarkXPress on an Apple G5 PowerMac
Set in 11/14pt Apollo
Printed and bound in Great Britain by
Page Bros, Norwich, Norfolk

To the memory of my parents,
Sean Mackey
1915 – 1986
and
Lyle O'Flynn Mackey
1916 – 1977

On a dark night
Kindled in love with yearnings
– Oh, happy chance!
I went forth without being observed,
My house being now at rest.

In darkness and secure,
By the secret ladder, disguised
– Oh, happy chance!
In darkness and in concealment,
My house being now at rest.

St John of the Cross, *Dark Night of the Soul*

Contents

Author's note

Aubépine is not the real name of the village where my monastery was. I have changed its name and the names of the nuns to protect their privacy.

All quotations from the *Dark Night* are from *St John of the Cross, Dark Night of the Soul*, trans. E. Allison Peers (Burns & Oates, 1976). Used by permission.

All quotations from *The Spiritual Canticle* are from *St John of the Cross, The Spiritual Canticle and Poems*, trans. E. Allison Peers (Burns & Oates, 1978). Used by permission.

Still Crazy After All These Years, words and music by Paul Simon; © 1974 Paul Simon. Used by permission of Music Sales Limited. All rights Reserved. International Copyright Secured. *Something So Right*, words and music by Paul Simon; © 1973 Paul Simon. Used by permission of Music Sales Limited. All rights Reserved. International Copyright Secured. *Slip Slidin' Away*, words and music by Paul Simon; © 1977 Paul Simon. Used by permission of Music Sales Limited. All rights Reserved. International Copyright Secured. *Train in the Distance*, words and music by Paul Simon; © 1983 Paul Simon. Used by permission of Music Sales Limited. All rights Reserved. International Copyright Secured.

Bible quotations, unless otherwise indicated, are from the New Revised Standard Version (Catholic Edition) (Oxford University Press, 1999).

Acknowledgements

The following persons have, in different ways, helped this book to see the light of day: Una Collins, a great English teacher who gave all her pupils a love for the language and its literature and who taught me that every piece of writing should have a beginning, a middle and an end; Susan Knight, whose Creative Writing class gave me the confidence and the focus I needed to get started; my brother Liam, who encouraged me from the beginning, who read every chapter as it was written and whose constructive advice and comments hugely improved the text; Brendan Walsh of DLT, who wasn't afraid to take a chance on me; his colleagues Helen Porter and Hannah Ward by the immaculate care they took with a nervous debutante's manuscript; Sarah John by her wonderful illustrations; Irene Dunne, Mairead Flanagan and Maeve Kerney who read the typescript and offered helpful suggestions, and my sisters, Clare and Eileen, who encouraged me in this as in everything else I do. Thanks to each and every one of them. And finally, thanks to the nuns of 'Aubépine', without whom this book would never have been written and whose friendship remains one of the great blessings of my life.

Prologue

Aubépine! The name still evokes longings deep in my heart. I have only to close my eyes, find that inner space of silence, and I am back there once again. I smell the peculiarly evocative scent of the hawthorn that gives the little village its name and I walk once more under an April sky across fields whose ditches are a riot of bursting white blossom. I turn at the brow of the hill where it falls to the plateau, and look back at the yellow huddle of buildings almost hidden in the forest. In winter, the same forest shimmers with hoarfrost and with snow, so that in my mind Aubépine is always dressed in white like a bride.

I remember that the sun shone one morning in early February 1996 when the little hill looked as beautiful as ever and I was at last in the place where I had so longed to be. I sat at the window of my cell looking out at the novitiate garden which ran down to meet the edge of the forest, where sometimes wild boar were seen in the late evening. The view was one of the most peaceful I had ever seen and I wondered what was wrong with me. Because I did not feel peaceful. Unexpected and unwelcome pictures kept flashing into my mind with the suddenness of a television news item: pictures of my family realising that I was never coming back, pictures of my apartment in Luxembourg which I would never see again, pictures of my quiet evenings alone with Mozart, Handel or Paul Simon playing on the stereo. A song kept running through my head: 'Still crazy after all these years'. Why did that suddenly seem so appropriate?

Oh, Aubépine! You were winter and summer, dawn and dark night, joy and anguish, death and birth!

1

PART ONE

'I met my old lover in the street last night'

Paul Simon, *'Still crazy after all these years'*

Chapter 1

Three years before Aubépine, I was working as a lawyer at the European Court of Justice in Luxembourg and living in a small cream-coloured apartment block on the Rue de Bourgogne. The french windows of my white-tiled living room opened onto a balcony that overlooked the forest of Beggen. I had furnished the balcony with a small white table and two chairs and surrounded it with window boxes filled with pink and red geraniums. Here I would sit with my book in the long summer evenings, a glass of wine in hand, while Paul Simon's reedy, nasal voice floated out on the evening air. His voice perfectly suited the moment and the mood, and I still remember those songs: 'You can call me Al'; 'Diamonds on the soles of her shoes'; 'Rene and Georgette Magritte with their dog after the war'; 'Train in the distance'. The book would frequently be laid to one side as a tranquillity that was only in part the effect of the wine and the music took hold of me, and I would spend hours gazing across the treetops at the distant hills, lost in no particular thought that I could identify. The hills would slowly darken as, one by one, lights began to come on here and there, like the eyes of animals shining in the night. The CD would come to an end, and I would be lost in the night and in the silence.

One such evening – it was in June – I had installed myself as usual in my favourite deckchair, Paul Simon playing on the stereo. I was looking forward to getting into my book; new books have always filled me with the same sense of anticipation that I feel when, pleasantly hungry, I sit down to a well-spread table. I read the first few pages. They weren't holding my attention, although the book had got good reviews, and several people I knew had read it and liked it. This inability to concentrate on what I was reading was happening more and more frequently during that summer, and I couldn't understand it. Concluding that it was the fault of the book, I returned inside to look for something else. Crouched before the bookshelves, I pulled out volume after volume, but nothing appealed. Then a purple-covered, rather thick paperback at the back of one of the shelves caught my eye. I took it out. It was *The Spiritual Canticle* of the sixteenth-century Spanish mystic, St John of the Cross, in the E. Allison Peers translation. I hadn't looked at it for years. Idly, I opened it at the page where the full text of the famous poem is set out, and read the first lines:

> Whither hast thou hidden thyself, and hast left me, O
>   Beloved, to my sighing?
> Thou didst flee like the hart, having wounded me: I went
>   out after thee, calling, and thou wert gone.

I can't easily describe what happened next. How is it possible to feel shattered by the desolation of bereavement and, at the same time, bewildered by the joy of reunion after long absence? In the same moment that I found what I had lost, I realised for the first time that I had lost it. Tears were streaming down my face as I went back to the balcony carrying my treasure, and even now I don't know whether they were tears of joy or of sorrow. But I know that they were healing tears, and I sat up very late that night, riveted by the magic of the words I was reading and of the promise they contained.

> My Beloved, the mountains, the solitary wooded valleys,
> The strange islands, the sonorous rivers,
> The whisper of the amorous breezes.
>
> The tranquil night, at the time of the rising of the dawn,
> The silent music, the sounding solitude, the supper that
>   recreates and enkindles love.

'I met my old lover in the street last night'

That night, as Paul Simon might have put it, I met my old
Lover.

Chapter 2

And yet, in another way, you could say that I hadn't met my Lover at all that night, but instead, that I set out in search of him. It was not the first time I had done so, which is why I can say that he was my 'old' Lover. I was sixteen when I made my first acquaintance with the Christian mystics John of the Cross and Teresa of Avila, and enraptured then by the same poem that was again holding me in thrall, I had set out on the great quest armed with all the assurance and self-confidence of youth, not knowing that those weapons above all were too heavy to carry on the journey.

Believing at that time that the only possible route was the one followed by St John of the Cross himself, I had, at the age of eighteen, entered an enclosed contemplative monastery of the Carmelite order. At first, all had gone well, but little by little it became evident to me and to those around me that the strictly enclosed life of a Carmelite in the 1960s was going to prove too difficult for me. The changes brought about by the Second Vatican Council had not yet taken place, and the life that we lived behind our grilles was much the same as that lived by Teresa of Avila in the sixteenth century. It was a physically difficult life, but more than that, it was a life that allowed no development of individual talents and personalities. Conformity was very important, and those who succeeded in living happy and fulfilled lives were persons of stronger character than I am.

But I didn't want to give up. This was what I had longed for during the last two years of secondary school; it was the path to the secret place that St John of the Cross had written about, 'the place where he [well I knew who!] awaited me, a place where none appeared'. I wanted to find that place and I knew of no other route. I battled on until the strain became too much, and my health broke down. This way, of course, I had an 'excuse' for leaving; I wasn't turning my back on my vocation or on my quest, I was being forced to leave by my own health. But although this may have provided me with an excuse that allowed me to leave without losing face, it didn't wash with my own conscience, and I left the convent with an appalling sense of guilt.

Back in the world again, I could find only one way of coping with this guilt, and that was not to think about God at all. This was difficult at first but, like anything, it became easier with practice. I continued to do the things practising Catholics did: I went to Sunday mass, and to confession every so often, but I no longer prayed because it was too painful. And because nature abhors a vacuum, the life that I was emptying of God gradually filled up with things that were not God. I began to drift and to lose the impetus that had made me set out in the first place.

Externally, things were good. I recovered fully, studied law, qualified as a barrister and began to practise. I had new friends, a pleasant lifestyle, absorbing work. But, as the years wore on, I gradually turned aside from the road that seemed to lead nowhere, and found more interesting pathways that led, as it then seemed to me, somewhere. Among other places, they had led me to take up a three-year contract in the research and documentation division of the European Court of Justice in Luxembourg. And on that night in 1993, the truth that hit me with such force that it almost killed me was that in fact during those years I had given up the quest, and had stopped seeking the Beloved. But I learned an even greater truth too that night, and that was, to quote again the great Spanish mystic, that if the soul is seeking the Beloved, how much more is the Beloved seeking the soul! Try as I might to forget him, he never forgot me.

So I think I can say that I did indeed meet my old Lover that night, but only for an instant. Yet that instant was long enough to revive in me all the dying and dead embers of my first love, and I set out once more on the quest, full of renewed hope, but without the self-assurance that had marked the first journey almost thirty years earlier.

The next morning, I woke with the feeling that the entire world had changed its appearance. Even the colours of the sky and the trees seemed more vivid, and as I walked along the Rue de Beggen on my way to the Court, I was enclosed in a little cocoon of happiness that I felt must be visible. Anyone who has been in love will know the feeling.

But naturally, the initial exhilaration didn't last, and when it had worn off a bit, a fairly concrete difficulty began to make itself evident. It was simply this: what should I do next? Of course, anyone with any experience at all of these things would have advised me to pray and meditate regularly, but I didn't know anyone I could ask, and for some reason, spending time in prayer (as opposed to reciting prayers) never occurred to me. The prayer habits of my early days in Carmel had long since been lost. I felt, however, a need to equip myself with tools, as it were, so I bought a Bible and a breviary. I began my new life by reading a little from the Bible each day, and by reciting morning and evening prayer from the breviary. But it wasn't enough. By the beginning of the following year, I knew I needed some sort of total immersion, and the idea of going on a short retreat came into my mind.

There were a number of places in and around Luxembourg that I could visit. There was, for example, a retreat house attached to the Benedictine monastery of Clervaux, in the Luxembourg Ardennes, a place of singular beauty and tranquillity, which I knew quite well. But somehow, since this epiphany had been triggered by the writings of one of the great Carmelite mystics, I felt I would like to make my retreat in a

Carmelite monastery (houses where Carmelite nuns live are called 'monasteries', not 'convents'). I had a book called *Guide to the Monasteries of France* and it contained a number of possibilities. I toyed for a while with the idea of a Carmelite monastery in Cannes (a nice combination, I felt, of spirituality and hedonism) but in the end fixed on one in the little village of Aubépine. I had never visited the part of France where Aubépine was located, but it sounded idyllic – rolling hills, miles of forest, vineyards and pastureland. With some trepidation, I prepared for the retreat, arranging leave from the Court and booking a place for a long weekend at the monastery guesthouse. The letter I received in response, signed 'Soeur Claudine', seemed welcoming, but I wasn't quite sure what lay ahead.

In mid-March, I set off by train from Luxembourg. I had to change trains at Metz, an attractive town in Alsace-Lorraine just over the French border, and as there was a wait of about two hours, I wandered into the town to have lunch. Metz is only about forty minutes' train ride from Luxembourg and I knew it well, as I often went there with friends for shopping on Saturdays.

The day was uncharacteristically warm and sunny for March; there was already a hint of summer in the air. I had a holiday feeling as I strolled towards Galleries Lafayette and the little café where I always had lunch when I was in Metz. Deciding it was warm enough to sit outside, I sat down at a table with a view of the passing crowd, and as I ate my omelette and salad and sipped my *vin rosé*, I began to feel that I could find more enjoyable ways of spending the coming weekend than by enclosing myself in a monastery in the depths of the country. The more I thought about what I was going to do, the more alien it seemed, and I came very close to abandoning the project entirely and finding a hotel in Metz instead. However, I suppose I was a little bit afraid that I might later regret not having risen to the challenge, so, deciding to regard it as an adventure – and one that could subsequently be dined out on – I paid my bill and set off back to the railway station.

The rest of the journey passed without incident until I got off the train at the station of the provincial town nearest to Aubépine. At the information booth in the station I was told that a bus would be leaving for the village within the hour. When it came, it was full of schoolchildren returning home to the outlying villages, and I squeezed in beside two very vocal 10-year-old boys. After about twenty minutes of edging through the evening traffic, we left the town behind us, and were in open countryside. The land was rich, and much of it had been ploughed in preparation for the spring sowing. The last rays of the sun lay long over the fields. The landscape was beautiful, but lonely, and all my fears woke again.

After a while, a new anxiety made itself felt. Where on earth was the monastery? We had passed the last village ten minutes earlier, and nothing was in sight except trees and hills and fields. The bus was more than half empty too, most of the children having already got off. I made my way up the coach to the driver, and asked if he knew the monastery.

'The Carmel of Aubépine? No, never heard of it. Maybe some of the kids would know.'

He roared a question down the bus. It provoked an instant, noisy and varied response; some children, who appeared to be residents of Aubépine, assured the driver shrilly that no monastery existed there; others loudly disputed this, but gave it as their opinion that we had already passed it. Finally, by dint of shouting louder than everyone else and adopting the additional expedient of approaching the driver (somewhat in the manner of American attorneys approaching the Bench during a trial), a faction of two managed to make itself heard. These boys had inside information; their families personally knew the nuns, and they had actually been to the monastery. This seemed promising, but upon interrogation, although they knew roughly where it was situated, they had no idea how I might get there. They were, however, adamant on two points: the bus did not pass it, and it would be impossible to get there without a car.

'But *where* is it?' I asked in despair.

'Voilà!' they said, pointing ahead to a hill which had just come into view. 'It's right at the top', they added, with some relish.

I made a quick decision. 'OK,' I said, 'let me out here.'

The driver stopped the bus at the foot of the hill. He, the boys and I looked at the hill in silence. Dusk was beginning to fall. A road of sorts wound its way up part of the hill, before it disappeared from sight.

'Perhaps you could take a short cut across the fields,' suggested the driver doubtfully.

I looked up at the richly ploughed furrows and then down at the rather dressy shoes I was wearing.

'No,' I said, 'I don't think so.'

I unloaded my luggage and stepped off the bus, thanking the driver for his assistance. Tooting his horn, he drove off. As the bus turned the corner, my two young friends leaned from the window, waving.

'Bon courage!' they called. 'Bon courage!'

I felt I was going to need it.

Chapter 3

In retrospect, the tin of biscuits I had bought in Metz for the nuns seemed not to be such a good idea. The plastic bag that contained it knocked painfully against my leg at every step as I trudged up the hill in the deepening dusk. I had no idea how long it would take to reach the monastery. Everything was very silent. A city-dweller all my life, I was unused to the total stillness of twilight in the country and I was unnerved by it. As the light faded, I could see less and less of my surroundings, but for the first five minutes or so the path seemed to follow the edge of the ploughed field I had seen from the bus. As I turned a corner the field vanished and as far as I could make out, a wood now bordered the path at the right-hand side, with open country at the left. Far below I could see the lights of the town I had left. A train hooted as it left the station. The sound was very distant. I felt very alone.

As the path began to climb more steeply I began to feel uncomfortably warm, and my misgivings deepened with every step. Putting down my luggage, I halted for a moment and reviewed my options. I could go back down the hill, and catch the bus into town as it returned from Aubépine. The problem was, it might already have returned; I had no idea how far away the village was. But I did know that there was no other bus until the morning. The alternative was to continue climbing, possibly get lost in the dark, and perhaps be attacked by some wild animal or worse. I didn't seem to have much choice; so, picking up my burdens again, I continued to climb.

By now, to add to my other troubles I was becoming increasingly short of breath. The path turned another corner and mounted sharply. Suddenly, I saw a light shining ahead. I had arrived! But no, as I got nearer, I saw that I had reached a fork in the path. To the left, a track led towards a large farmhouse from which shone the light I had seen. A road to the right wound on upwards into darkness and a small signpost indicated that the monastery was in that direction. Sighing, I plodded wearily on.

As things turned out, there wasn't much further to go. After a little, I came to an open gate set between low pillars. Peering at the notice affixed to one of the pillars, I managed to make out the words 'Bienvenu au Carmel d'Aubépine, lieu de prière et de silence'. Passing through the gates, I entered a broad avenue, still bounded by woods on the right-hand side. The way had levelled off, and progress was easier. My breathing began to return to normal as, rounding the last bend, I saw before me a low huddle of buildings. The main building, which was facing me, was two-storey. No lights showed in any of the windows. Adjoining it at right angles to the left, mounting a slight slope, was a stepped terrace of three narrower buildings. No windows at all could be seen on the part that was facing the drive. Another building to the extreme right was clearly identifiable by its soaring roof as a chapel.

I approached what appeared to be the entrance to the main building. It was a glass door across which heavy curtains had been drawn on the inside. I searched unsuccessfully in the darkness for a doorbell, and was looking around in some puzzlement when my eye was caught by something swaying gently in the breeze a little above my head, to the right. It was a bell, about six inches in diameter, and attached to it was a long chain. I pulled this; the bell produced an unexpectedly loud and unmusical jangle. It did not, however, produce any response from within. I tried a second time with no better result.

And then I remembered the chapel. As it seemed likely that the nuns were there, I decided to investigate.

*

15

The singing met me as I opened the door; then I saw the nuns. They were arranged in two semi-circular rows to the right of the altar in the sanctuary. Dressed in brown robes and wearing black veils, they stood, hymn-books in hand, chanting vespers, and for a few moments I saw nothing else.

I was utterly appalled.

As I look back now after so many years, I realise that I was experiencing my own inability to understand the meaning of community. I had travelled so many millions of light miles away from my teenage years that, when I looked at the little group in the sanctuary, what I saw were women who had lost their identity, and the sight froze my blood. At the same time, I felt an inner resistance that was later to become very familiar and which I now recognise as my own fragile sense of identity rising up in outrage to protest against becoming a member of the herd. At that moment, however, it manifested itself as a sense of superiority and even arrogance. I pitied the nuns.

The first shock over, I moved into one of the pews and began to take in more of my surroundings. The chapel was simple and beautiful, painted in soft natural shades of cream and stone, modern in design and minimalist in decor. The roof, supported by heavy wooden, ladder-like beams that creaked and cracked alarmingly with changes of temperature, soared to a point above the centre of the building. The nuns' chairs in the sanctuary were divided from those of the congregation by a low iron altar-rail. And the whole place was filled with the high pure sound of the singing.

Vespers came to an end. As the nuns filed out, I realised that someone was trying to attract my attention from behind. Turning round, I saw a small elderly nun, with bright eyes and a lively manner. In her brown habit, she looked a little like a robin and I liked her immediately. She introduced herself as Soeur Annette, and told me to follow her.

Leading me out of the chapel and across a gravel path at the side of the main building, she pushed open a door which I hadn't noticed when I arrived. This was the guesthouse – *l'hôtel-lerie* – of the monastery. At first sight, it reinforced the general impression of bleakness. We were in a fairly small *salle*, poorly lit by the weak bulbs hanging in a sort of cluster from the high ceiling. In the centre of the red-tiled floor was a long refectory table, covered with oilcloth and surrounded by straight-backed wooden chairs. A glass jam jar in the middle of the table held a miserable little bunch of wild flowers long past their sell-by date. To the left of the doorway was a curtained alcove. The curtain was partly drawn and I caught a glimpse of a heavy old-fashioned kitchen sink. A stone staircase covered in red drugget rose up into darkness.

Switching on another feeble light, Soeur Annette led me up the stairs, chatting away incomprehensibly as we went. My French was not very fluent, and unless people spoke slowly I hadn't a hope of understanding what they said. I caught the odd word here and there, and gathered that she was apologising for the fact that she hadn't been at the guesthouse when I arrived. By now we had reached my room. It was tiny. Like the *salle*, it had cream walls and a red floor and was furnished in a spartan manner, but to my weary eyes it seemed more cheerful than anything I had seen so far. It was a nest, and I had already decided that I was going to cocoon myself, for I could think of no other way of surviving the weekend. As Soeur Annette turned to go, I handed over the tin of biscuits. She was very pleased.

'Nous sommes tous un peu gourmet!' she beamed.

I felt a bit better. At least one of the nuns was human!

Chapter 4

The next few days passed in a blur of new impressions and rapid mood swings. After the initially unfavourable impact made upon me by the nuns, I tried to ignore them and to get on with the business that had brought me there. A good night's sleep brought a change of outlook, and the *hôtellerie* seemed a much more cheerful place next day. The *salle* bathed in morning sunlight was almost beautiful in its cream and red simplicity and I wondered why I had found it bleak the night before. Breakfast, consisting of a huge bowl of steaming, milky coffee and slices of crusty baguette with butter and homemade plum jam, completed my sense of well-being and I began to look forward to the next few days.

The whole place was conducive to peace and inner silence. Although other visitors were staying in the *hôtellerie*, a rule of silence at mealtimes meant that this was not a distraction. I attended all the religious offices sung by the nuns and little by little was able to concentrate more on the beauty of the singing than on the bleak lives I imagined they were leading.

But the greatest benefit bestowed on me by those few days was the rediscovery of prayer and meditation. Sitting in the chapel during the long periods of silent prayer which the nuns passed there morning and evening, I began to discover a place of inner stillness. This experience greatly resembled my evening tranquillity on the balcony in Luxembourg, but whereas then the experience was one of vagueness and even emptiness, now the overwhelming impression was of presence. Strange longings awoke in me at those times. Little by little, something deep in the

18

dark caverns of my being was stirring, waking, beginning to breathe. I wasn't sure what it was, or how I should deal with it, but some inner certainty led me to try not to interfere.

> Without light or guide, save that which burned in my
> heart.
> This light guided me more surely than the light of noon,

St John of the Cross had written, speaking of the delicate awakening of God in the human soul.

The weather was warm, sunny and spring-like for the first two days. I spent most of my free time in the open air, exploring the woods and fields around the monastery. Those were the times I felt happiest and most at peace; I could forget about the nuns and their awful lives of imprisonment, and become one with nature. I was in one of the most beautiful regions of France, where lush vistas of rolling hills stretched on every side. My soul expanded; I felt I was beginning to breathe properly for the first time.

One of my favourite walks followed a track that began just below the monastery. The track led deep into the woods, and I revelled in the luscious damp aroma of the undergrowth. Sap was rising everywhere, and new birth seemed to be all around. After about a quarter of a mile, the woods opened out to a clearing from which there was a panoramic view of the countryside below. Someone (one of the nuns, I wondered?) had provided a convenient sawn-off tree trunk at the best vantage point in the clearing and this became my place of refuge.

But on Sunday morning the weather changed. I woke to the sound of torrential rain on the roof and as I drew back the thin brown curtains and looked out at a grey, desolate, drenched landscape, the weary day stretched before me in all its interminable drabness. My spirits plummeted again. How on earth was I going to fill up the time? I couldn't pray all the time. Then, cheering up slightly, I remembered that I'd brought some books with me against just such an eventuality. The books posed a new dilemma, however. They were not spiritual books; indeed, they were thrillers and detective stories – the stuff of distraction. So far, I had felt no need to open them, and as I took them out now, they seemed alien to the sort of life I was temporarily leading. Frowning, I laid them to one side, intending to come back to them when breakfast and the morning offices were over.

When I returned to my room some hours later, the peace that was the aftermath of my new periods of prayer wrapped me about like a blanket. Instead of opening an Agatha Christie, as I had intended, I picked up the French Bible with which the room was equipped. I opened it at random, and my eyes fell upon chapter 2 of the Song of Songs.

The words I saw there seemed to burn themselves into my mind and into my heart without any effort on my part – 'Viens donc, ma bien aimée, ma belle, viens!' –

> Arise, make haste, my love, my fair one, and come away;
> For now the winter is past, the rain is over and gone.
> The flowers appear on the earth;
> the time of singing has come,
> and the voice of the turtle-dove is heard in our land.
> The fig tree puts forth its figs, and the vines are in blossom.
> They give forth fragrance.
> Arise, my love, my fair one,
> And come away.
> O my dove, in the clefts of the rock,
> In the covert of the cliff,
> Let me see your face,
> let me hear your voice;
> For your voice is sweet,
> and your face is lovely.

Flooded with happiness, I was conscious at some deep level of responding to an invitation. Like the experience on the balcony in Luxembourg, two things seemed to happen simultaneously: the response was given at the same moment that I became aware an invitation had been issued. The question of a refusal never arose; yet I knew that my choice was freely made. Translated into ordinary language, I felt I was being called to belong in some very particular way to the one who was calling. I knew now that much more was being asked of me than simply making a place in my life for prayer and spiritual reading: what had just happened called for a commitment to a person in as real a sense as if someone had proposed marriage.

And indeed, the Christian mystics would say that something akin to a marriage proposal had taken place. St John of the Cross and St Teresa of Avila, for example, both speak of a mystical state that they call the spiritual marriage. They believe it to be the highest mystical state to which a human being can aspire in this life and they say that all those who embark upon the mystical quest are invited to it. It is not always the case that one actually experiences the invitation, but it is no less authentic for not existing at a felt level.

The happiness that resulted from this experience coloured the remainder of the short time I spent in Aubépine and I was even able to regard the nuns with a kindlier eye when I next saw them in the chapel, huddled together in their amorphous little group. Presumably they had rich inner lives, I thought, even if externally they seemed so lacking in individuality.

Back in Luxembourg the following week, everything seemed as before, yet nothing was the same, and nothing would ever be the same again. At first I was completely disorientated by what now seemed the frenetic, lunatic activity of everyday life, in contrast with the sane and tranquil rhythm of life in Aubépine. Little by little, however, life resumed its normal patterns of work and leisure – and, of course, prayer. But now prayer was very different to what it had been in what I had begun to think of as 'pre-Aubépine' days. It was no longer simply a matter of reciting prayers from the breviary – although I continued to do that too, seduced by the beauty of the psalms and finding that they frequently gave expression to the inexpressible things that were happening inside me. Instead, it became something that I needed in the way that I needed food. I discovered that there is an inner hunger, just as there is a physical one.

Returning home from the Court after a busy day, I would rush through the various chores that needed to be attended to, have a hasty meal and then go to my bedroom, sit at my desk and close my eyes. For a short while, I would be conscious of sounds inside and outside the building: birds singing, traffic passing on the street, the high heels of Madame Schmidt in the apartment above tap-tapping their way across the floor. But gradually these would fade, the inner noise and bustle would slowly hush and the little babbling stream that was myself would lose itself in a deep, enriching ocean.

Such were the early, peaceful days of my prayer life, and at that time I believed that was how it would always be. I thought I had found God, and my only concern was how to fit this intense spiritual activity into what I thought of as my 'everyday' life. I had a lot to learn. The days would come when prayer, deeper than ever, would be a refuge from the storms that raged both without and within, and later again, prayer itself would become agonising, as my inner and outer lives waged war on one another. But for now, I luxuriated in the calm that, though I did not know it, presaged the storm to come.

Chapter 5

The months wore on, and summer came round again. It was time to think of holidays. I always spent part of the holidays at home in Ireland with my family, and the remainder in Nice. This year, however, Nice just didn't seem right, but I couldn't think of anywhere I wanted to go instead – except, of course, I realised with a sudden shock, Aubépine. And then I thought: well, why not? Why not spend my summer holidays there?

The matter was quickly arranged. I would spend ten days in Aubépine in July. Not yet totally converted to the idea of a holiday that didn't contain the usual holiday things of sight-seeing and meals in nice restaurants, I arranged to spend the final four days of the fortnight touring the region round about.

Since my previous visit, I had given a lot of thought as to how best to respond to the invitation I felt had been made to me when I read the passage from the Song of Songs. Finally, I decided to make a private commitment to a life of celibacy, as this seemed to best accord with a total commitment to God. I chose a date during my current visit to make this commitment, and in preparation, in order to symbolise in a concrete way what I was doing, I had bought a plain gold ring. I made the commitment, not in the chapel at Aubépine, but in a church in the nearby town, en route to the monastery. Thus, I arrived at the Carmel already wearing the ring, and aware that I had taken an irrevocable step. I was very happy.

The second visit to Aubépine was very different from the first.

This time, I knew what to expect, and the nuns no longer raised my hackles. Soeur Annette greeted me like an old friend, her wrinkled old face happy.

'La voilà, la grande fidèle!' she cried. The faithful one? Clearly, it was unusual for anyone to make two visits in such rapid succession!

During this visit, I met for the first time the Soeur Claudine who had replied to my first letter. She was at that time the prioress of the little community and was in her mid-fifties. Tall, well built and warm-hearted, with her fresh-faced complexion she had something of the Celt about her; she reminded me of the women of the West of Ireland. She was very easy to talk to and after a few minutes you felt you had known her all your life. Somehow, you felt you could tell her anything and she would never be shocked. I could understand why the community had elected her as their prioress. Talking to her and to Annette, I realised how wrong I had been in thinking that those who lived in the community had lost their identity. Annette and Claudine were very much their own women.

But it was my meeting with Soeur Véronique that finally totally changed my opinion. I had already noticed her in the chapel. She was petite and vivacious, with a wide smile and piercing brown eyes whose brilliance even the old-fashioned spectacles she wore could not conceal. Although the hair that showed from under the front of her veil was steely grey, her thick eyebrows were still black, and I thought that she must have been stunning as a girl. At that time in her late fifties, she was still a very attractive woman.

I met her one day at the entrance to the guesthouse, where she was waiting to let in some workmen. She engaged me in conversation, obviously intrigued as to why I had come twice in such a short time. I found myself telling her a little bit about what had been happening to me.

'You're searching,' she said sympathetically.

'Well, I suppose I am,' I replied. 'I'm really not sure how to fit a life of prayer in with the life of a lawyer. There's a constant tension between the two parts of my life.'

'If God is calling you to a life of prayer, he won't make it impossible for you to respond,' said Véronique. 'Just be patient – with yourself, above all, but with those around you too.'

Her perspicacity astonished me, for I was indeed impatient, anxious for my dilemma to be resolved. Later I told Annette I had spoken to Véronique and been very impressed by her. The old nun was not surprised. Véronique had been prioress before Claudine, she explained. Indeed, she had been re-elected on a number of occasions, but their rule sensibly provided that there should be a change of superior at least every six years. She could, however, be elected again after a break of three years. She was a very talented woman, said Annette. 'C'est une femme trés douée!'

When the holidays were over, I had much to occupy my mind. These nuns were not at all the mindless group that I had at first believed them to be. I couldn't get them out of my mind. Little by little, the idea began to grow that living in such a community – living in *that* community – would be the solution to the problem of how to reconcile prayer with everyday life. The more I thought about it, the more attractive it seemed. But I was forty-five years old; I had a career. And above all, I had tried this before without success. Was it sensible to think of risking so much now? What would I do if things didn't work out?

I wrestled with the problem for months. I didn't know anyone whose advice I could ask. There were times when I was sure that the only thing to do was to join the community and there were other times when I felt that it would be madness to take such a step. One night, I dreamed I was climbing a narrow wooden stairs. I knew (in the way one knows these things in dreams) that the stairs led to the novitiate in Aubépine. About four steps from the top, I was suddenly thrust backwards with extraordinary violence by what felt like two hands against my chest. Greatly shaken, because I couldn't see anyone, I began to climb again. The same thing happened a second time. There was a frightening sense of an evil presence and of hatred directed at me personally. Once more I began the ascent and as I neared the place where the presence seemed to lurk I began to lose my breath with terror. As the hands thrust once more against my chest, I woke, bathed in sweat, my heart pounding. The dream haunted me for days.

Matters continued like this for the rest of that year. In the spring of 1995, I went to Aubépine for Holy Week and Easter. Annette greeted me with the news that they had held elections in February, and that Véronique was once more prioress. I felt unaccountably cheered by this news.

The guesthouse was full. Among those staying there was a French woman, Michèle, in her early thirties. We fell into conversation, and she told me that she was thinking about entering Carmel and had come to Aubépine to get advice. She had talked to Véronique, who had encouraged her, but had advised her to pray about it for another year and then to come back and talk to her again. Michèle seemed very happy, but her story filled me with conflicting emotions. I envied her certainty about what she wanted, and at the same time, the old bogey of loss of identity in the communal life rose up again to haunt me. I went to bed with a feeling of loss, but I could not identify what it was that I had lost.

The next morning, it was perfectly clear to me that I too should seek Véronique's advice. I couldn't see why I hadn't thought of it before. I made up my mind to ask to see her that day. And yet as the day wore on, something kept holding me back. For one thing, I was afraid I wouldn't be able to explain myself properly in French. And I was afraid of what she might advise. On the one hand, I was not ready to hear that I ought to leave everything and join the community; on the other, I was equally afraid she would tell me that the life clearly was not for me.

In the end, I decided to write to Véronique when I got back to Luxembourg. The letter took a long time to compose. By this time, the most important thing to me was to carry out whatever seemed to be God's will for me, and so I tried to be absolutely candid in what I told Véronique about my life up to that time. Written down on paper, the life I had lived, while not very different from that of many of my contemporaries, did not seem to me to have much in it that would recommend it to the prioress of a community of contemplative nuns. With a sinking heart, I posted the letter and tried to leave the outcome to God.

Three weeks passed without any reply. My sister came on a visit from Ireland and in spite of my efforts to conceal my anxiety she grew suspicious. On her last night, she asked if something was wrong. I hadn't wanted to say anything at such an early stage, but when I realised that she thought I was concealing the fact of a serious illness, I decided to tell her the truth. She has since told me that she wasn't sure whether she wouldn't have preferred the serious illness! Seeing how upset she was, I began to reassure her that it was most unlikely that any community in its right mind would accept me, but she wasn't convinced.

My sister returned to Dublin the following morning, and when I got back to the apartment from seeing her off at the airport, I found a letter from Aubépine: Véronique wanted me to come to see her. I went down the following weekend. Waiting in the little monastery parlour, I had a sense of something momentous about to happen. Véronique arrived, beaming, and I immediately felt welcomed and at ease. She wasted no time in pleasantries but got straight down to business. We first discussed some of the things I had told her about my life, and she quickly dispelled any fear that they might of themselves pose obstacles. My age, of course, was a factor. She knew, as indeed did I, that the older one is the more difficult it is to make radical life changes. She did not believe, however, all else being equal, that it would be impossible.

'So,' she said, after about thirty minutes, 'what do you want to do?'

The question took me by surprise. I hadn't expected to be put to an election at this point. I had thought we might have an initial conversation that day, and then that I would write to her from time to time, and maybe come and discuss the matter further in a few months ...

'I don't know.' I said lamely.

Véronique was a little impatient. 'Well, would you like to come and do a *stage* here – live with us and share our life for a few weeks, to see how you would like it?'

I found myself saying yes, and before we parted I had agreed to take all my leave from the Court at one go, and come to spend the month of August with the nuns.

PART TWO

'Still crazy after all these years'

Paul Simon

Chapter 6

I arrived to begin my stage in the middle of a heat wave. The nuns who had assembled to greet me seemed to shimmer in the August afternoon. I was a bundle of nerves; this was evident to everyone and they did their best to put me at my ease. After the initial greetings, Véronique handed me over to the care of Soeur Marie-Jeanne, the novice mistress, who would be my guide to the mysteries of community life throughout my stay. Of all the nuns, it was Marie-Jeanne who was to have the greatest influence upon me. I had of course seen her before. She sat near Véronique in the chapel and indeed at first I used to confuse the two of them, as they were roughly the same height and build and both wore glasses. At that time in her early fifties, she was small (almost all the nuns were small when viewed from my height of five feet ten inches), fair, round-faced and given to flashes of wit and infectious bursts of merriment. Musically gifted, she was burdened with an artistic temperament that caused more pain to herself than to anyone around her. It most frequently manifested itself in an easily wounded sensibility, and she waged a fierce war against this small flaw for as long as I knew her. She was a charming, loveable, generous, deeply spiritual woman, and I regard her enduring friendship as one of the great graces of my life. Those members of the community who had had the good fortune to make their novitiate under her care were utterly devoted to her.

Marie-Jeanne brought me first to the room (or cell, as it was called) that was to be mine for the month. It was a pleasant surprise. Situated at the back of the monastery, it was more spacious than I had expected. Its most striking feature was a window running from floor to ceiling, giving a view of the novitiate garden and the woods which surrounded the monastery. The prospect was green, tranquil and conducive to prayer. The room itself had the ubiquitous cream walls and red floor; it was simply furnished with a narrow, brown-covered bed, a plain wooden table and a stool. To the left of the doorway was a washbasin and to the right a curtained alcove containing shelves and a rail with a few wire coat-hangers. Over the whole room hung an aura of peace, and my inner agitation began to quieten.

The next few days were spent in becoming accustomed to the rhythm of community life, a rhythm which took its key from the liturgical seasons. I soon discovered that the nuns' entire life was lived in the awareness of the presence of God. This was something that seeped almost imperceptibly into my consciousness and, as the days passed, I began to feel more and more certain that this was the only way in which one could truly live a life of prayer. Everything helped. Five times a day the nuns assembled to sing the Hours of the Divine Office: the office of readings (or vigils) for the following day at 9 each evening; morning prayer (lauds) at 7 the next day; midday prayer at noon; evening prayer (vespers) at 6; while the beautiful and peaceful office of night prayer (compline) was chanted in darkness at 10 p.m., ending the day with a plea for God's blessing – 'May the Lord grant us a quiet night and a perfect end.'

Every day began with a celebration of the Eucharist, often attended by members of the public, who made the long early morning journey out from the town in order to join the nuns in their daily worship. And then there were the periods of silent contemplative prayer for which my soul hungered. Each morning I woke in the happy knowledge that I had only to go downstairs, enter the darkened chapel and lose myself for the first hour of the day in that wordless encounter. I could not get enough of it

I was like an addict waiting for the first fix, and I couldn't have borne it if anything had intervened to prevent it.

And of course the nuns worked too: they had to support themselves. They grew their own vegetables; the large garden, aided by the green-fingered and masterly hands of Soeur Solange, produced artichokes, green beans, courgettes and lettuces of all kinds. Eggs and milk came from a nearby farm, but everything else had to be purchased and Marie-Jeanne drove into town every Wednesday in the community's white Renault Clio to do the weekly shop at the local Carrefour. To finance all of this, the nuns did various things. Some of them worked at the traditional monastic tasks of needlework and book-binding; others (mainly the younger ones) had diversified into *l'informatique* and were much in demand by university students for the typing and formatting of theses. There was also the usual work involved in running a sizeable house, and as not all of the nuns were in the first flush of youth, more of the housework and the upkeep of the woods and garden fell on the younger ones. The nuns varied widely in age. At that time, of the eighteen nuns who made up the community, four were over eighty, two in their seventies, three under thirty-five and the rest between forty and sixty.

The time passed rapidly and happily as I got to know the various members of the community. Initially, the fact that they were all dressed identically and were more or less the same height made it difficult to distinguish one from the other. But after a little time spent in their company, I wondered how I could ever have thought they were alike. Even Véronique and Marie-Jeanne, who in the beginning had seemed like twins to me, I now realised bore absolutely no resemblance at all to each other except in the most superficial way. Their personalities were totally different. Véronique's smiling exterior, I soon discovered, concealed a deep personality. No matter how warmly she greeted you, you were conscious that something of herself was held back. Her embrace was always disconcerting: she would open her arms wide to you and you would start to walk into them, only to find yourself held at arm's length, your shoulders gripped with a strength that did not allow you to come any closer. But with Marie-Jeanne what you saw was what you got. She was totally incapable of guile and you always knew where you were with her. Her embrace was a bear-hug; she took you immediately to her heart and you knew that you were loved.

Of the others, Solange, brown-faced and weather-beaten, was the gardener; dressed in trousers and gumboots and an old apron made of sacking, she could be seen in all weathers digging, hoeing and weeding, in spite of the fact that she was already in her seventies. She loved her garden and for her it was an extension of the chapel, a further dimension of prayer.

Thérèse was one of the young ones. Early thirties, dark-haired, creamy-skinned and striking-looking, she was a peace-maker by nature, always ready to give in to Marie-Paule when that young woman's opinion differed from her own. The two were the same age and were the best of friends, although differing widely in temperament, character and physical appearance. Thérèse was one of those calm, confident people who are always trusted by their elders; the sort of person who is appointed a prefect at school and in whose hands the status quo will always be safe. Everyone liked her.

Marie-Paule was blonde, slim and a born leader, a talent that she did not have much opportunity to exercise in the community. As one of the youngest members, she had to accustom herself to being led rather than to lead, and many were the battles she waged against herself in this regard. She was one of the world's movers and shakers and in another life would most certainly have been a highly successful career woman. Her temperament was active and practical, and in this again she differed from the rather dreamy Thérèse. She found an outlet for her energy in outdoor work; she loved to clear brush in the forests, to experiment in the little carpentry shop and to drive the community tractor. She was at her happiest when she was rendering some service to the community, which she loved with a fierce devotion. I admired her immensely, because I recognised that her battles could well be my own. Of all the nuns, she was the one I felt I would have made friends with if I had met her in another context, and her presence in the community was to me a further proof that the love of God and the quest for him overcame all obstacles.

There was one postulant, incongruous in her trousers and tee shirt in the midst of the brown-robed, black-veiled nuns. Angèle was twenty-four and had been a maths teacher in a Lycée in the North of France. Tall (the only member of the community who matched me in height) and very thin, she gazed at you peacefully from behind her glasses with large myopic eyes. Earnest, determined and somewhat reserved, she seemed already to have navigated her way through the difficulties and rules of community life in a way that I felt I would never be able to match. She greeted every project proposed by Marie-Jeanne in the novitiate with an enthusiasm that I was inclined to view with a jaundiced eye. Was it possible that she loved everything? Or was she so self-sacrificing that she was always able to overcome her own feelings? Either way, my own base nature found such constant good will an irritant, not least because it showed up my own considerable failures in this regard. I had to acknowledge that I found it hard to be outdone in virtue by someone young enough to be my daughter.

Life was not all prayer and work. Every evening, the sisters assembled for a period of recreation during which they chatted about the events of the day, or indeed about world events. Although they did not watch television or listen to the radio, they took a daily newspaper – the Catholic *La Croix* – and were generally well informed about current affairs. I found these periods of recreation difficult. The nuns sat around in a circle and only one person spoke at a time. It seemed a very formal way of relaxing and I never felt really at ease on these occasions. Much more to my liking was the *journée de noviciat*, or novitiate day, which took place during the second week of my *stage*. It was occasioned by the arrival of two postulants and their novice mistress from a Carmel near Paris, who came to spend a few days in the country. Marie-Jeanne decided that we would all go for a day's hike across country to a well-known place of pilgrimage about ten miles away.

We set off on a gloriously sunny morning, rucksacks on our shoulders. Claudine, whose motherly instincts found vent in spoiling the community and who loved to see *les jeunes* enjoying themselves, had packed a huge lunch for us; cold chicken, tomatoes, crusty rolls, chocolate, gingerbread and fruit. To wash it all down we had a bottle of white wine well insulated against the heat and a flask of coffee. The novitiate group was augmented for the occasion by Thérèse and Marie-Paule, who never objected to being counted among *les jeunes* when it was question of a hike or a picnic. The usual veils and robes had been abandoned and, in jeans and tee shirts, our group was indistinguishable from any other group of hikers abroad that day.

For me, that day was idyllic and the companionship perfect. We tramped along for about five miles before the first halt was called for a brief *pause café*. When we resumed, I found myself walking with Marie-Jeanne and, in the pleasant exchanges that followed, there was nothing to suggest the battleground our relationship would subsequently become. (But then, our relationship was not yet that of novice mistress and novice.) When we finally came within sight of the shrine, the whole company came to a halt and sang an ancient Marian hymn. Unexpectedly, my eyes filled with tears.

While we were at the shrine, the weather suddenly changed in the disconcerting way of French weather in August. The sun disappeared, angry violet clouds arrived from nowhere and the first rumbles of thunder were heard in the distance. In a frighteningly short time, the storm broke directly overhead with great violence. We ran for shelter to the tower of the ruined church, and there we crouched, one on each step of the spiral staircase while thunder roared, lightning flashed incessantly and the rain came down in torrents. It was all over within thirty minutes, but not before a nearby tree had been struck by lightning with a sound like a bomb exploding.

By the end of the third week, I felt I could never live anywhere else and I told Véronique I wanted to join the community. She was somewhat taken aback at the speed of the decision, given my earlier ambivalence, but I was absolutely certain and I wanted to enter as soon as possible. Véronique, however, was not anxious to rush things. She suggested I return to Luxembourg until Christmas and then come for a second *stage* of a month, with a view to finally entering on 2 February. I would have a space of two weeks between the end of the *stage* and that date in order to wind up my affairs in Luxembourg. And so matters were arranged.

The months passed quickly – too quickly, I sometimes felt. In November, I returned to Ireland to say goodbye to my family and friends. I spent a week in Dublin and it was a stressful time for all concerned. Nerves were on edge and emotions high. I thought it would never end. It was a sad and depressing visit and I returned to Luxembourg in low spirits. Finally Christmas came. The goodbyes at the Court seemed interminable, but finally I was able to leave and head once more towards Aubépine. The second *stage* passed off well; I made my formal request for admission to the community and was formally accepted. The low spirits in which I had returned from Ireland had not fully lifted, but I knew I was under a great strain and I was certain that all would again be well when I finally joined the community. I did, however, feel that I needed a short period of transition in which to ease my passage from one way of life to another, so I suggested to Véronique that I should arrive a few days early and spend them in the *hôtellerie*. She agreed, although she said this was unusual.

My last two weeks in Luxembourg were spent in a whirl of

activity, winding up my affairs, saying goodbye to friends and arranging for my furniture and belongings to be sent back to Ireland. At last the final day arrived. The removal van came and emptied my apartment. The phone, the gas and the electricity were cut off. I stood in the gloom of a January evening and looked around the cold, empty apartment. The balcony where it had all begun was desolate in the grey half light. No flowers decorated its rails, the white table and chairs had gone with the rest of the furniture. I was suddenly panic-stricken. Why am I doing this? I wondered. And then, from nowhere, came those words of St John of the Cross:

> On a dark night, kindled in love with yearnings,
> Oh, happy chance!
> I went forth without being observed,
> My house being now at rest.

Strangely cheered, I locked the door behind me and left the apartment for ever.

Chapter 7

I left for Aubépine the following morning, having spent my final night in Luxembourg in a hotel. Two Danish friends from the Court, Lisbeth and Kristian Knudsen, had invited me to spend the night with them, but I had not been able to bear the thought of any more farewells and wanted to be able to leave without any fuss in the morning. At Luxembourg railway station, I tried to still the almost unbearable fluttering in my stomach by pretending that this was just an ordinary visit to Aubépine, but it didn't work. In the train I felt like a ghost, as though I were no longer part of the life that was going on all around me. Looking out as we passed through a village, I saw a woman sweeping the steps of her house and was overcome by the realisation that this was just another ordinary day for so many people, while for me it was the end of the world as I knew it. When I got off the train at the little town near Aubépine, I walked the streets for several hours, trying desperately to feel part of life again. Finally, thinking that I might as well get it over with, I hailed a taxi and set off for the Carmel. But once I arrived at the *hôtellerie*, all was well again. With grateful relief I unpacked in the little red and cream room that seemed as much of a refuge as it had done on the occasion of my first visit. And as on that first visit, the peace of the place poured its balm over my battered and bruised soul and I relaxed and remembered why I had come. Prayer enfolded me in its embrace, and I knew I was where I needed to be.

Those days were unexpectedly beautiful for late January, mild and sunny; again, as on my first visit, I spent much of the time walking in the woods and fields of Aubépine. Véronique and Marie-Jeanne came to talk to me each day and their warmth and concern provided the final reassurance I needed.

On 1 February I wrote in my diary: 'On this last day in 'the world' the sun is shining everywhere – out of doors and in my heart.'

The next morning, I rose early, cleaned my room, packed my overnight bag and left it at the enclosure door, where Claudine would take it in later. Then I made my way in the darkness for the last time from the *hôtellerie* to the chapel for the hour of prayer. I was totally at peace and the time was spent in a commitment of the rest of my life to the God who I believed had called me. I remained in the public part of the chapel while the community recited lauds, and when it was over Véronique left her place and came to where I was. She looked at me for a moment, smiled, and then quoted the words from the Song of Songs that had meant so much to me: 'Come … for now the winter is past, the rain is over and gone.'

Getting up from my seat, I followed her and took my place among the nuns of Aubépine.

Later that morning, I sat at the window of my cell while the memories that I had tried to push away came flooding in. Where now was my peace? I couldn't pray. I could only watch helplessly while the unwelcome film of small joys I would never know again and of anxieties about my family replayed itself over and over in my imagination. The fact that the day was a *jour chomé* didn't help matters. A *jour chomé* is a feast day on which no work is done. The idea is that the nuns will have extra time for prayer and be better able to enter into the particular mystery the liturgy is celebrating. So I had nothing to do but pray: something that would normally have been a great luxury, but that today was totally the wrong thing.

The day passed somehow. The evening was a little better;

Angèle appeared at recreation dressed in the full Court robes of a French *avocat* – to make me feel at home, she said – and I tried to relax and enter into the spirit of the thing.

However, as on the occasion of my first visit to Aubépine, everything looked better the following morning after a good night's sleep. During mass, I was struck by the words of the Gospel: 'Anyone putting his hand to the plough and looking backwards is not fit for the kingdom of heaven,' and I prayed to be able to let go of all the things that were preoccupying me, all those unwelcome memories that were plucking at the skirts of my imagination.

Chapter 8

As a new postulant, I did not, for the first few weeks, have to rise with the rest of the community at 5.45 in the morning; instead, I had a lie-in until 7 and joined the nuns in time to recite lauds. This meant that I missed the hour of prayer that began immediately upon rising, but Marie-Jeanne told me that instead I could take an hour in my cell after breakfast. This hour rapidly became a time of refuge from an unexpected source of tension, which began to arise at breakfast time after the first few days.

Typically, I would become aware that Marie-Jeanne was attempting to attract my attention from her place across the refectory. I would resist raising my eyes as long as possible, but eventually I would crack and look up. Marie-Jeanne would immediately begin making signs to me to hurry up, pointing at the door to indicate that she wanted to speak to me outside (a rule of strict silence was observed in the refectory at mealtimes). This meant that she had some project that she wished me to undertake for that day. It was rarely something I liked; more often than not it was to help prepare the midday meal, an activity which, because of my lack of talent in that domain, was a source of stress and disturbance. For all that the slogan of that great mystic Teresa of Avila was constantly repeated in the novitiate – 'God walks among the pots and pans' – my own experience at that time was that I lost him in the kitchen. I hated it. Instant irritation and resistance would arise in me. I resented the disturbance; consequently, I began to resent Marie-Jeanne for causing it. I fought desperately against this unexpected rebelliousness. I told myself it was foolish and childish, but to no avail.

'Still crazy after all these years'

The hour of prayer in my cell thus became a refuge to which I could escape. Lost in that mysterious embrace, peace returned again. During those periods, I sought strength to resist the rebelliousness, and sometimes it came.

The days passed, one blending into the next so imperceptibly that sometimes I only knew what day of the week it was by the psalms of the Office. Lent began and the weather became colder – although it may simply be that it felt colder, because we were fasting. On the evening before Ash Wednesday, I was horrified to discover that the menu for the following day was black coffee for breakfast, potatoes puréed with water for lunch and watery soup for supper. Most of the nuns didn't even take the potatoes at midday. Throughout Lent, breakfast consisted of black coffee and dry bread. I missed the plum jam and milky coffee in the mornings. Sitting in the archive room in the afternoons, sorting and classifying old documents, I felt I would never again be warm. The late afternoon light was grey and chill. I hadn't seen the sun for weeks and I wondered how the others stuck it. However, in spite of all this, I felt peaceful.

> *Thank You for what you are beginning to show me, even though my heart keeps failing me. But when I turn to You, I have a moment of peace and of respite, because, since the beginning of this adventure You have given me the firm conviction that if You want me here at Aubépine You will supply everything that I need.*

Then one morning Véronique knocked at my door during my prayer time to tell me that she was anxious about me.

Chapter 9

A few days before, a notice had appeared on the community notice board. It announced that Père Jean Levêque would be coming to spend three days at the Carmel and anyone who wished to speak privately with him should fill in her name on the attached timetable. Père Jean was a Carmelite friar from Paris whom I had first met during my *stage* at Christmas. A profoundly spiritual man, he was much in demand as a spiritual director. I thought about putting down my name, but decided against it, as I had nothing in particular to discuss. Besides, one of the obligations of the novitiate was an hour's spiritual direction from the novice mistress once a week. I felt that was all I needed; indeed, I frequently felt it was more than I needed, as usually I could find nothing to say to Marie-Jeanne during these sessions.

The morning that Véronique came to see me, I had been feeling particularly at peace. I had managed to hold onto it even when Marie-Jeanne told me after breakfast that this would be a kitchen day. I was convinced things were improving. Véronique had been on retreat for the previous ten days and when she knocked at my door, I was at first delighted to see her. Things began pleasantly enough. We talked for a bit about her retreat. Then she said, still smiling her invariable smile, so that I was taken completely by surprise,

'I notice you haven't put your name down for a chat with Père Jean?'

'No,' I replied. 'I didn't feel there was any need.'

'Well, I think there's a great need,' said Véronique firmly. 'I was very distressed to see such a change in you when I returned from my retreat.'

Considerably taken aback, I asked her what she meant. She said that I seemed sad and depressed and not at all the person I had been. I assured her she was mistaken and explained that, on the contrary, I felt full of peace. She wasn't convinced. Greatly upset, I went to find Marie-Jeanne, only to discover that she had already discussed the matter with Véronique, because she too was concerned about me.

I was devastated by Véronique's visit and by the discussion with Marie-Jeanne. How could they – especially Marie-Jeanne – have got things so wrong? I brooded over it for days and little by little I began to wonder whether they, with their experience of the spiritual life, could see something that I could not. Was it in fact I who had got things wrong? This was even worse. If I was wrong about the peace that I had felt flooding over me the previous weeks, then how could I be sure of anything? Now everything was thrown into question, from the experience on the balcony in Luxembourg onwards. I sat in my cell and wept. Where was all this going? In the end, I knew that there was only one thing to do. I badly needed the advice of an experienced counsellor. I went downstairs, and wrote my name on Père Jean's timetable.

On the day appointed for my talk with him, I went to see him in one of the three parlours where the nuns met their visitors. As soon as I saw Père Jean, a slightly built, grey-haired man in his sixties, dressed in the brown Carmelite habit, I burst into tears. I was very embarrassed, but if Père Jean was taken aback, he didn't show it. Regaining my composure with some difficulty, I explained to him what had happened. He didn't say whether he thought Véronique was correct or not, but asked me about myself, and how I felt. I told him about the trouble I had in accepting Marie-Jeanne's breakfast-time instructions; it was a relief to get it out in the open. Père Jean was sympathetic and understanding. He pointed out that a change of lifestyle such as the one I had made must profoundly affect the psyche and that the older one was and the more set in one's ways the greater the shock to the system. He understood that Véronique's opinion had greatly shaken my confidence in my own history and he told me that it was important to cling to one's truth. I felt relieved when I left him.

The relief didn't last. As the days passed, I began to feel uneasy and self-conscious. Trying to convince Véronique that I was happy, I beamed at her every time I met her on the stairs or in the corridors. It didn't have the hoped-for effect. Véronique was more worried than ever.

'Such an artificial smile!' she said to me one day, her own smile for once a little clouded. 'There's no happiness in it at all.'

I tried to explain to Marie-Jeanne how all this was making me feel. In my anxiety to get this across to her, my French became more and more halting and I began to despair of ever crossing the chasm that seemed to have opened up between us. Marie-Jeanne was far from persuaded; on the contrary, she took the opportunity to tell me that other members of the community had expressed anxiety about me. In desperation, I asked what I could do to redress the matter. Marie-Jeanne thought for a few moments.

'Well,' she said finally, looking at me a little anxiously, 'perhaps you could try to participate a bit more, be a little more forthcoming at recreation for example. And you could try to conceal your repugnance for being disturbed – it's very off-putting, and some of the younger sisters especially are afraid to ask you for any help. You can be quite intimidating and even give the impression of arrogance at times.'

From that moment, my peace vanished. And yet, even as I write it, I am aware that that statement is not totally true. It would perhaps be more correct to say that from then on my life seemed to be lived on two levels. There was the felt level, where all was anxiety and worry about what the rest of the community was thinking about me. There was anger too at this level, that people could so misunderstand me as to find me intimidating; such an accusation had never before been levelled at me. But at a deeper level, something else was happening. Some part of me recognised more than a grain of truth in what had been said. It was true that I deeply resented anything that interfered with my peace and that this resentment manifested itself in very subtle ways that could well appear as – maybe was – arrogance. And amazingly, at this deep level, which was almost, but not quite, subconscious, I was aware that the peace flowed on like a sub-terranean river, untroubled by the rocks and boulders that constantly came crashing into it.

> *O Source of all peace, now I realise that when You became troubled and distressed in the garden of Gethsemane, it was this sort of inner anguish You experienced. And so, for the first time, really, I feel drawn to contemplate You in that garden; alone, anguished, needing the friends who weren't there for You. In spite of all the difficulties, this Lent seems to me wonderful; a journey through the desert with You to the Father.*

Nevertheless, the next few months were unhappy and stressful. I became painfully self-conscious and increasingly ill at ease with the nuns. The chaos of my thoughts and feelings found relief only during prayer, but this prayer was a far cry from the silent and blissful state I had known until then. Now when I commenced to pray, it was to look for strength and support in this unexpected battle. It was the only place where I felt totally understood and accepted and my reaction to that found expression in tears. This soon attracted further unwelcome attention from Véronique. Trying to blow my nose and wipe my eyes quietly in the silent chapel during evening prayer, I would hear her shifting uneasily in her chair. It wasn't long before she raised the matter directly. What was all this crying about? Why was I unhappy? I explained that I wasn't crying from un-happiness, but from the relief I felt in the acceptance and under-standing I was experiencing. Véronique was not impressed. Now prayer itself became a source of stress as I fought – usually unsuccessfully – to remain at a superficial level so that the tears would not begin. I wondered where it would all end, and longed for a respite. And then, in the most unexpected way, one came.

Chapter 10

It was April. Holy Week and Easter had come and gone, but all that this meant to me that year was that Lent with all its bleakness was finally over. The days were getting longer and the weather was getting a little milder, and somehow I didn't feel quite so bad. The whole community was making preparations to celebrate the golden jubilee of Soeur Marie-Cécile's profession. There was to be a solemn mass, to which her family was invited and, later that evening, the community would hold its own celebrations with music and perhaps some amateur theatricals. In the novitiate, there was much discussion as to what we could do to contribute to the proceedings. I racked my brains and came up with the idea of teaching some of the younger nuns an Irish dance, a proposal that was enthusiastically received.

It was a very long time indeed since I had done any Irish dancing, but I had a fair idea of the basic movements of the four-hand reel. So I enlisted Thérèse, Marie-Paule and Angèle and began to teach them the dance. We rehearsed for days and I started to enjoy myself and even to look forward to the great day. However, on the evening before, I began to have severe cramps in the back of my legs. I put this down to the unaccustomed moving about on tiptoe and hoped it would improve before the actual performance the next evening.

But the next morning saw no improvement. My left leg, in particular, was extremely painful. I could walk only with difficulty and I wondered how on earth I would manage to dance that evening. I tried a few tentative steps and to my relief discovered that once I rose on my toes the pain subsided, so that it was actually easier to dance than to walk.

It was a beautiful spring day. The weather had been getting gradually warmer since Easter and suddenly the garden of the monastery was ablaze with scarlet tulips and golden-yellow daffodils. A faint green haze surrounded the branches of the trees in the woods as the leaves began to unfurl and every morning the chapel was filled with an exuberance of birdsong. My own spirits rose with the barometer and, in spite of the pain in my leg, things seemed to be looking up. The jubilee mass was beautiful. Marie-Cécile had chosen all the music, and after the communion this old nun, who was so severely incapacitated by arthritis that she was confined to a wheelchair, read aloud a personal testimony in which with a complete lack of self-consciousness she expressed her joy at having given herself so totally to the contemplative life for the past fifty years. As I listened to her, I felt my own troubles fall into perspective and my heart lifted. After the mass, Marie-Cécile's extended family was entertained to a special celebratory meal in the *hôtellerie* and from inside the enclosure, we could hear the shouts of her young grandnephews and -nieces at play in the garden. The cheerful sound of the children's voices on the evening air carried me back to my own childhood; I found it strangely comforting.

Finally, the hour arrived for our own party. Marie-Paule and Thérèse had been busy all afternoon and the austere community room had an unusually festive appearance. Balloons were everywhere, and along one wall, a long trestle table covered with a white cloth held all the little presents we had made for Marie-Cécile. We assembled to await the lady of the moment, who arrived in style but with unexpected speed, her wheelchair rather too enthusiastically propelled by Angèle. When the laughter had died down, she began a solemn inspection of the presents, accompanied along the length of the table by Véronique. Everything delighted her; she admired them all.

Then the entertainment began. The community had several

musically talented members: Thérèse played the violin while Angèle was an accomplished flautist and together with Marie-Jeanne they had rehearsed a wonderful baroque trio for flute, violin and harpsichord. Marie-Jeanne, not having access to a harpsichord, did great things with an electronic keyboard. Several people sang or recited, and finally the moment came for *la danse irlandaise*.

The *corps de ballet* were dressed in the closest approximation to Irish costume that we had been able to put together by raiding the miscellaneous garments left in the attic by postulants after they had become novices. Each of us had managed to get hold of a white shirt and, for the rest, we were arrayed in an assortment of kilts and checked skirts, with wide green ribbons tied around our waists as cummerbunds. A motley and colourful crew, we took our places; Angèle and I with joined hands raised high facing Marie-Paule and Thérèse. Marie-Jeanne put the cassette I had given her on the recorder, the music commenced, and we were off. Forward, back, cross to your opposite partner … I was getting into the swing of it now. I skipped higher. As I executed a fast cross to Thérèse, I felt a sudden violent pain in my left leg, and with a horrible sound like a whip cracking, my Achilles tendon snapped in two.

Chapter 11

It was midnight when Véronique, Marie-Jeanne and I arrived at the hospital. In the car on the way there, greatly struck by the coincidence, I had told them about a dream I had had the previous night. I had dreamt that I had been bitten on the left hand by a snake and the hand had swelled up and turned black and blue. This was the part of the dream that so impressed me, because my left leg had by now swelled up and, like my hand in the dream, had turned black and blue. Then the dream had taken another turn. I thought I was going to die because of the snake bite and I went in search of Véronique to tell her so. But I couldn't find her, and the dream ended that way. When I told them this part of the dream, Véronique was upset.

'I feel I've failed you,' she said. 'I wasn't there for you when you needed me, and that's what provoked that dream. But things will be different from now on.'

As our car pulled up at the hospital entrance, a nurse came out with a wheelchair.

'What on earth happened to you?' she asked.

'Well,' I began, 'I was dancing ...'

'Dancing!' The nurse, a stout, comfortable-looking woman of about sixty, looked at us in disbelief. Her surprise was understandable. No doubt it was not every Saturday night that three nuns presented themselves with injuries suffered during a dance. Feeling a hysterical desire to giggle, I wondered whether she would try to sniff my breath.

We had to wait some time for the doctor to arrive, and when he did, elegant in *tenue de soirée*, it was clear that we had dragged him away from a pleasant evening. He was not at first in the best of humours and hurried through the formalities with some impatience. But when I spoke, he stopped short.

'You're Irish!' he exclaimed. 'I recognise the accent.'

From then on, he was my friend. Breaking into English, he explained that he and his wife loved Ireland; they spent almost every summer there. His wife would be enchanted to hear that he had an Irish patient! She would most certainly come to visit me! Mais oui! Véronique and Marie-Jeanne listened in bewilderment to this exchange. They could not follow any of it, but it was clear to them that there had been a complete turnaround in the doctor's attitude. When he had left, I explained.

'Well,' said Veronique drily, 'don't let him or his wife persuade you to do any Irish dancing for them!'

I spent a week in the hospital. Apart from an operation on the Monday to repair the tendon, it was, as far as I was concerned, a total holiday. I relaxed fully for the first time in weeks and being at a distance from the community allowed me to get a lot of things into perspective. Véronique and Marie-Jeanne came to visit me almost every day and on the days they didn't come we spoke on the phone. I had other visitors too; the community's chaplain Père Dubois came, as did Marie-Jeanne's great friend Yvette, who was one of those stalwart women who befriend communities of nuns and become invaluable. And as promised, Dr Borgi's wife came, and proved to be just as much a lover of Ireland as her husband. During this time of repose, I began to remember again what it was that I loved about the community and to look forward to returning.

> How mysterious Your ways are! You have removed me from the constant struggle and given me a time of respite. I have such a strong sense of Your intervention in my life. Show me now how to respond.

After a few days, I began to learn to walk on crutches. This was more difficult than I had expected, but the great thing was that

I was able to walk at all so quickly. There had been two options for the repair of the tendon; one involved the leg being put in plaster and remaining immobile for six weeks, the other (which the surgeon chose) was to insert a temporary brace, and this allowed me to begin walking almost immediately.

On the morning I was due to go back to Aubépine, one of the nurses came to say goodbye.

'You're lucky to be so well,' she said. 'Your poor colleague has got an infection in his leg, and is back in bed. He won't be going home for another week or two.'

My colleague? I was puzzled.

'Frère Christian, the Trappist monk who broke his Achilles tendon,' the nurse explained. 'Didn't you know about it?'

'No,' I said, greatly intrigued. 'Tell me more!'

'But', said the nurse, 'he came in the same night as you did. He snapped his tendon while he was dancing. We all thought you had been dancing together!'

It was no wonder, I reflected, that the nurse who met us on the night of my arrival had been scandalised. I decided I would have to meet this comrade in distress, so, having enquired where he was, I presented myself on my crutches in his room where he was in bed with his leg raised. The poor man seemed a little taken aback by the unexpected visit.

'You don't know me,' I began, anxious to put him at his ease, 'but we are bound together by a mystical link ...'

He looked more nervous than ever at this opening, so I hastened to explain before he summoned a nurse to have the madwoman removed. He greatly enjoyed the joke. Unbelievably, his accident had also happened during jubilee celebrations. An old monk in the monastery was celebrating his diamond jubilee and Frère Christian had been demonstrating a Breton dance. Several months later, I received a package from him in the post, containing a copy of his monastery's newsletter. Some artist in the community had drawn a cartoon depicting Frère Christian and myself jiving wildly together, each waving a crutch in our free hand.

Véronique and Marie-Jeanne came to bring me home. As we drove back to the monastery, I saw that the leaves had fully opened on all the trees while I had been in hospital. The sun was shining from a cloudless sky as we drove along the country road that led to Aubépine, and when Marie-Jeanne opened the window of the car the air that drifted in was warm and perfumed with growing things. The hedges were snowy with hawthorn and birds sang deliriously everywhere.

'C'est beau chez nous!' said Marie-Jeanne happily and I agreed. Home was beautiful indeed.

Chapter 12

The nuns had got a wheelchair for me. When I protested that I could walk perfectly well with the aid of crutches, Véronique explained that they were thinking of the fairly long distance that separated the novitiate from the community room, chapel and refectory and they had decided that I ought not to exercise the leg too much at first. Remembering the speed at which Marie-Cécile had entered the community room the evening of her jubilee, I was somewhat apprehensive to learn that Angèle had been deputed to wheel me around. She assured me, however, that she was a reformed character and that we would proceed at a pace befitting my injuries and my grey hairs.

'Less of the "grey hairs"', I warned her. 'You won't be twenty-four for ever, you know!' It was good to be back.

Since I could not go upstairs and since there were no bedrooms on the ground floor (except in the infirmary, and I wasn't really a candidate for that) my belongings had been temporarily moved to a room in the *hôtellerie*. Changes had been made in the novitiate too. A small corner of it had been screened off, so that I could remain there in some privacy during the periods I would normally have spent in my cell.

Dr Borgi had warned that we should ring him immediately if the leg showed any sign of swelling. Just before I went to bed on the first evening back in the monastery, I saw that it had become twice the size of the other leg. I went in search of Claudine, who among her many other tasks, fulfilled the function of infirmarian in the community, and after she had tut-tutted over the appearance of the leg, she went off to ring Dr Borgi. I hobbled

56

back to my new room in the *hôtellerie*, got into bed with some difficulty and was just drifting off to sleep when the door opened and Véronique, Marie-Jeanne and Claudine all arrived together, armed with a huge pile of pillows. Dr Borgi had instructed that I should stay in bed for the next few days and keep the leg raised, to avoid the danger of a clot.

Before going to bed, I had said goodbye to Marie-Jeanne and Marie-Paule, who were due to leave early next day to attend a three-day conference for Carmelites in Paris. But next morning I was woken by a knock at the door, followed by the entrance of what appeared to me in my half-asleep state to be a veritable procession. It was headed by Véronique, bearing a tray with croissants, butter and jam. She was followed by Marie-Jeanne and Marie-Paule, while Claudine, carrying a coffee pot, brought up the rear. They crowded into the tiny room and burst into song: 'Café au lait, au lit!' they sang. Milky coffee in bed!

'We wanted to say goodbye again before we left,' Marie-Jeanne explained, laughing at my bemused expression.

Surrounded by all this solicitude and with so many testimonies of the nuns' affection, I wondered how I could ever have felt misunderstood and isolated. Annoyed with myself for having wallowed in self-pity for so long, I resolved to try to relax more and not to take too seriously the small misunderstandings that arose from culture clashes and language difficulties.

> *I need the courage that only You can give. Help me to take up community life again with generosity. Help me to remember that it is for You, not for myself, that I have come here.*

During the period of convalescence that followed my return to the monastery, I struggled to keep the resolution I had made. It was easy enough at first while I was being cosseted and treated like an invalid and no demands were being made upon me. But as my physical health improved and I began to take up various duties again, the old reluctance and resistance began to make itself felt once more. I couldn't understand it. I had come to live a life of prayer and of self-forgetfulness, but I was twenty times more wrapped up in myself than ever I had been before I joined.

St John of the Cross had the answer, if only I had the eyes to see. In the intense life of prayer that I was now leading, I was opening myself up to the light of God. Contemplation, as he explains it, is that light shining on the dark places of the human soul or psyche. God is total purity; the human upon whom he is shining is not. The light is so intense that it is perceived as darkness and oppression and it lights up the hidden places of the human spirit, bringing into view the deeply rooted neuroses and warped tendencies that we are all so adept at concealing even from ourselves. This vision of ourselves can be very hard to take, but unless it is accepted and lived through, we can't make any progress in the contemplative life. For these things are brought to light, not to horrify us, but so that they may be healed by the burning light that is shining upon them.

For, says St John of the Cross,

> this Divine purgation is removing all the evil and vicious humours which the soul has never perceived because they have been so deeply rooted and grounded in it; it has never realised, in fact, that it has had so much evil within itself. But now that they are to be driven forth and annihilated, these humours reveal themselves, and become visible to the soul because it is so brightly illumined by this dark light of Divine contemplation.
>
> (*The Dark Night of the Soul*, Book II, Ch. X)

Yes, they were revealed all right, and not only to myself. There was, for example, the matter of the bell.

PART THREE

'It took a little time to get next to me'

Paul Simon, *'Something so right'*

Chapter 13

The monastery's two bells were fixed high on the roof of the chapel, and were rung by means of long ropes which hung down into the chapel itself, behind the altar; the larger was rung for all the community offices, while the smaller was only used on those special occasions calling for joyful bell-ringing, such as Christmas Eve and Easter, when both bells were rung together (more or less) by perspiring novices. There were two different methods of ringing the big bell: a slow tolling of one note, used for the Angelus and for some parts of the office, and a steady, rhythmic, back-and-forth ringing, where the clapper hits first one and then the other side of the bell. This latter method was always used to summon the nuns to the hours of silent prayer. The bell-ringer changed each week, with the appointment of the new ringer read out in the refectory at the Saturday midday meal ('pour sonner la cloche, Soeur Marie-Paule'). Some weeks after my return to full community life, Marie-Jeanne told me that I would soon be appointed to take my turn, but that first she would show me how to do it, as people sometimes had difficulty with the tolling. I was delighted; I had been longing to try my hand at it since I had arrived.

I proved to be hopeless. Contrary to expectations, I had no problem with the tolling; it was the steady ringing that defeated me. Time after time, Marie-Jeanne would take the rope in her two hands, pull down hard to set the bell swinging and then relax into a rhythmic up-and-down movement of her arms which produced a lovely two-tone peal. Then I would take over, and the bell would take on a life of its own. In the contest for control between the bell and me there was no doubt at all as to who was winning. When I started the procedure by pulling down hard, as Marie-Jeanne had done, the bell began a wild swinging, producing an unpleasant and unruly clanging. Or indeed, worse again, it produced no sound at all, as I wrote at the time to my friend Sheelagh in Ireland, describing a bell-ringing effort made in full view of the whole community, plus assembled members of the public:

> I reduced the community, who were assembled for evening prayer, to hysterics – not to mention the six or seven members of the public who were in the chapel. There is nothing more hilarious to behold than someone swinging with great might from the end of a bell-rope, growing purpler and purpler in the face and producing nothing but a great silence. The inner panic and growing horror this produces in the bell-ringer is something else, and I was almost in need of medical attention at the end of a three-minute session of silent gymnastics. No bell rang for prayer that evening, and I'm no longer allowed to perform that particular manoeuvre. The novice mistress and I rehearse secretly, all doors locked.

The first couple of times Marie-Jeanne and I rehearsed, we were both amused by the peculiar results I achieved. It wasn't quite so funny the third and fourth time round; I was becoming frustrated by my inability to master the thing, while Marie-Jeanne was clearly beginning to suspect that I could do better if I put my mind to it. As ever, Marie-Jeanne's apparent readiness to believe the worst where I was concerned caused me to seethe inwardly. I began to be obsessed by the bell and the arguments I had in my head with Marie-Jeanne about it were many and violent.

Matters finally came to a head one day early in June. Marie-Jeanne had made up her mind that I was going to learn how to ring the bell once and for all. We were going to practise, she announced, and we would not stop until I had mastered it. I followed her into the chapel, looking around nervously to make sure it was empty. My sister was staying at the *hôtellerie* at the time, having come to spend a few days with me and I definitely did not want her to witness the performance that I was sure would follow.

The lesson began.

'Pull down firmly,' said Marie-Jeanne.

I pulled down firmly. The bell rocked and clamoured wildly.

'Again,' said Marie-Jeanne, her lips pressed tightly together.

I pulled again.

'Now!' she instructed. 'Relax your arms – up, down, up – I said *up*!'

Desperately I pulled and pushed, my ups and downs wildly out of synch with Marie-Jeanne's. What I needed was to be left alone so that I could concentrate. If only she would be silent for a moment and let me think.

'Down. *Down*, not up!'

'Will you stop and let me think!' I yelled. 'I'll never get the hang of it if you keep talking!'

There was a sudden appalled silence. Marie-Jeanne stared at me, two vivid spots of colour in her cheeks. Then she turned on her heel and walked away.

'Marie-Jeanne, no! I'm sorry, please come back!' I ran after her and grabbed her arm.

She turned to face me, but shook my hand off. I saw that she was near to tears.

'I was trying to help you,' she said quietly. 'I've given up time to come with you to practise the bell and the only thanks I get is to be told that I disturb your concentration. Do it alone then. You always think you know better than anyone else how to do things. It's impossible to teach you.'

I had no answer. This time I didn't try to stop her when she turned to go, and I stood for a long time where she had left me.

Chapter 14

Things couldn't continue like that, of course; something had to give. I apologised to Marie-Jeanne and she accepted my apology, but I knew that she was deeply hurt. She saw my behaviour at the bell practice as a rejection of her help, not only in that area, but in many others. I wanted to put things right, but didn't know how. The stress caused to our relationship by the bell affair provoked other disagreements and misunderstandings. And during all of this, something was happening to my heart and to my face. They were both slowly freezing. The ice in my heart caused a pain in my chest that never lifted and that interfered with my breathing; there was, in the most literal sense, a weight on my heart. The ice spread to my face. I couldn't smile. I wanted with all my heart to smile at Marie-Jeanne, and I couldn't.

After yet another dispute, I felt a great need for some space. I thought how easy it would have been to cope with disagreements like these if I were not in the monastery. I could go for a walk, or ring a friend. I could read a book, I could watch a film ... There were a thousand and one means of distraction; most of us need not live a moment longer than we want to with the pain of the small vicissitudes of daily life. It was different here in the hothouse atmosphere of the monastery; it was impossible to get away.

And yet, was it? Suddenly it came to me: the Prairie – a small field situated at the farthest limit of the monastery property, where sometimes we went for picnics. Its greatest attraction from my present viewpoint was its seclusion: one entered it by pushing through a heavy growth of brambles and going down a steep incline. The field itself was at the bottom of the hill, and once you were there you were invisible to anyone passing through the woods above.

It was 9.30 in the morning and it was the time allocated for manual work. My particular duty that morning was to clean the oratory. I did so at speed, and found I had a whole hour to myself. I set off through the garden into the woods and made my way down the hill to the field. There I sat on a flat stone in the sunlight, gradually soothed by the warmth of the air and the peace of that silent, secluded place. Little by little, my anger and resentment began to fade. I thought of all that Marie-Jeanne had done for me since my arrival, her undoubted affection for me, the many occasions on which she had willingly broken her busy schedule to discuss some problem that had arisen for me. I thought of her constant good humour in the novitiate and of all that she tolerated from both Angèle and myself. I knew she did not always understand the jokes I made; the Irish sense of humour is often rather obscure to others. Sitting there in the Prairie, I felt a huge desire to begin again, to try to break the deadlock that had arisen and to get back to the comfortable relationship I had had with her during my two *stages*. Getting up from my stone, I decided I would go to see Véronique and ask her advice. It had been a long time since I had had a good chat with her.

As it turned out, Véronique was busy all that day and it was the following day before I had a chance to speak to her. It was 16 July, the feast of Our Lady of Mount Carmel, one of the biggest feast days in the Carmelite calendar. It seemed a good day on which to turn over a new leaf. I found Véronique in her office, busy with the mountain of paperwork that always surrounded her. Although she greeted me with her usual smile, I thought I discerned a certain coolness in her voice, but I was too anxious to get on with what I had to say to pay much attention to it. She listened to my story in silence. When I had finished, she asked,

'Where did you go yesterday morning at 9.30? I saw you walk past the window of my office.'

For a moment I was puzzled; then I remembered my visit to the Prairie. I explained. Véronique looked at me thoughtfully. As usual, I found it impossible to guess what she was thinking. I wasn't left long in doubt.

'Did you really think that you could just walk off like that, when according to the timetable you had a duty to fulfil?' she asked.

'But I cleaned the oratory,' I protested. 'The rest of the time was free.'

'No,' said Véronique quietly. 'That's precisely where you are making a mistake. Your time is no longer your own and you don't seem to have realised that at all. You are now living by a rule; part of the discipline of our life here is that you can no longer exercise the sort of independent choices you would have exercised in the world. You can't just go off and have space when you need it. There are no distractions in this life. The journey you have begun towards union with God takes so much longer if you can step off the path every time the climb becomes a bit difficult.'

She said much more, all of it to the same effect: I had entered upon the ascent of Mount Carmel, and I must take it seriously or leave.

I was a mass of conflicting emotions. Burning resentment at what seemed to me to be constant and unnecessary surveillance fought with a giddy sense of being on the edge of a sheer precipice. Self-preservation won; I told Véronique I would change, and I realised a fundamental decision had been made. I asked her what I should do to try to repair the situation with Marie-Jeanne, and she softened a little.

'I suggest you simply tell her you have realised that everything has got out of hand and that you want to make a new start,' she said. 'I think you'll find that Marie-Jeanne will be more than willing to meet you half way.'

I left Véronique's office feeling as if I had narrowly escaped some great disaster. I immediately went in search of Marie-

Jeanne and found her in the sewing room where she was at work on one of the beautiful liturgical vestments that were her specialty. She looked up when I called her and I was struck to the heart by the resigned expression on her face. How had things between us come to such a pass?

'Marie-Jeanne,' I said hesitantly, 'I'd like to talk. Have you a few moments to spare?'

And as always, she didn't hesitate. When it was a question of the needs of someone under her charge, Marie-Jeanne never thought first of herself, although I knew that she was, as usual, snowed under by the demand for liturgical vestments.

We went outside. The sky was that dazzling blue that one finds only in continental Europe and the garden shone in the morning sun. Already, although it was only 10.30, the heat was of an intensity that in Ireland would only be felt at mid-afternoon during a heat wave.

We made our way to the place the nuns had christened Kerith, in memory of the prophet Elijah, always honoured as the true founder of the Carmelite order. According to the Book of Kings, it was beside the brook Kerith that Elijah went to live when a great drought fell upon Israel. There he was fed by a raven, and drank from the brook until it dried up.

Our Kerith was not a brook at all; it was a small glade surrounded by trees. Angèle had carved out a flight of earthen steps leading down to it and banked them with stones. Her university degree had been in engineering, and it had come in useful for the purpose. We had put some wooden seats there and in fine weather it served as an extension of the novitiate. Even I had contributed to the making of Kerith; I had painted its name on a piece of wood, which I had varnished and nailed to a tree near the steps. I had also placed pots of trailing sweet pea (grown from seeds sent by a friend in Ireland) on the steps, and their perfume permeated the hollow.

Marie-Jeanne sat down on one of the wooden seats and I sat beside her. For a while, neither of us spoke. The silence of the garden was broken by a thousand small sounds: birds chirped lazily in the trees, bees hummed, crickets whirred in the grass, leaves rustled in a faint breeze. I watched a small lizard idly flick his tail as he basked at the edge of one of the steps, limbs spread-eagled.

'Marie-Jeanne,' I said finally, 'I want to start again.'

After that, it was easy. She had only been waiting for some such surrender on my part to come to meet it with all the generosity of her nature. By the time we stood up to leave, a new leaf had been turned.

From that moment, something changed inside me. The weight that had been on my heart lifted, and I began to feel again something approaching the happiness that I had known during my early visits to Aubépine. Nothing seemed difficult any more, and the summer days that followed were resplendent with promise.

> The Bride has entered into the pleasant garden of her
>   desire,
> And at her pleasure rests,
> her neck reclining on the gentle arms of her Beloved,

wrote St John of the Cross in *The Spiritual Canticle*. During that heavenly summer of 1996 it seemed to me that he was right.

Chapter 15

Then began a period of light and happiness, when all doubts fell away and all resistance seemed to have evaporated. Like the darkness I had previously experienced, it reached down into my subconscious – or perhaps it began in my subconscious and manifested itself externally, I don't know. One evening during prayer, I began to wonder, not for the first time, who or what this God was, to whom I had so committed my life. I didn't doubt that he was Love, but I wondered what Love might look like, if you were to meet a being called Love face to face.

The old childhood images of God had long gone. They had been replaced at different times with different images, but lately my experience had been that of 'unknowing', familiar to most people who embark seriously on a life of prayer. In other words, while the old images of God had disappeared, nothing new was coming to replace them. This is of course an authentic experience, because the human imagination cannot provide us with any appropriate image of God; nevertheless, human nature finds it difficult to accept this. We always want to know; 'unknowing' is a very alien experience.

The Old Testament provides us with a vivid example of this in the story of Moses. Moses, we are told, talked with God as a man does with his friend. He went into the inner sanctuary of the Temple daily to speak to God and when he came out he had to cover his face with a veil, because it shone so brightly after this celestial conversation that his fellow Israelites could not bear to look at him. One would have thought that such conversation would be more than enough for anybody, yet Moses was not satisfied. He wanted to *know* this God to whom he spoke so familiarly, and so he prayed, 'Lord, show me your face.' And God replied to Moses that he would hide him in a hollow of the rock and pass by him, but that Moses would only see his back after he had passed. 'You cannot look upon my face', God told him, 'or you will die.'

During prayer that evening, I made a similar request: 'Who are you? Show me! Let me see your face.'

And then it seemed as if the brightness of my inner being intensified until it was total light. The light was youthful, and it *rejoiced* in its youth. I realised with a great shock that God is young.

God is Light, God is Youth, God is Joy.

Around this time too I had another vivid dream. I dreamt I was walking in the woods below the monastery, when I came to a steep hill. A rope rail had been fixed to posts all the way up the hill so that climbers could assist themselves by pulling themselves up (there was in fact a slope with a rope-rail in the monastery woods, but the dream hill was much steeper). As I began to climb the hill, pulling myself up by the rope, I saw that there was a thick mist ahead. I knew I would have to pass through that mist and I was afraid, because I knew that in that mist I would meet whatever it was I had met on the novitiate staircase in the earlier dream. I wanted to go back, but a voice called out: 'Go on! God has delivered you!' Terrified, I pulled myself up inch by inch, resisting with every step, but advancing all the same, until I came to the edge of the mist. And then I was in it, with a roaring in my ears and a horrifying and suffocating sense of evil presence. Equally suddenly, I was out again on the other side, in sunlight and blessed sweet air, running effortlessly down the far side of the hill with that sense of exhilaration remembered from running downhill in childhood, where one's legs took on a life of their own and one felt one could run for ever.

Now that I was no longer in a constantly embattled state, I could devote my energies to life in the novitiate. We were an oddly assorted trio. Angèle, who had entered three months before me, was twenty-four. I was forty-eight, while Marie-Jeanne was only a few years older. It was difficult for her to find a balance in her attitude towards Angèle and me. Angèle, on the other hand, was never wholly comfortable with a fellow postulant who was old enough to be her mother. As for me, well, sometimes I felt I was acting the role of a postulant in a badly directed play. I was often unsure of my moves and still more often unsure of the script, which seemed to keep changing. Angèle always seemed to know exactly what to do, whereas I regularly put my foot in things. We were uneasy bedfellows as we struggled along together throughout that summer.

Postulancy can last for anything from ten months to a year and a half. One misty day in October, I was in the garden weeding Solange's bean rows when I saw Marie-Jeanne and Angèle coming down the path towards me smiling and waving. They had good news: the community had voted to accept Angèle for her *prise d'habit*, or taking of the habit, the event that marks the moment when a postulant becomes a novice. Angèle was overjoyed, her normal reserve completely abandoned. I was delighted for her and then for the first time began to wonder about my own *prise d'habit*. In December, I would be ten months in Aubépine, but I thought it unlikely that I would be accepted so soon — if ever, indeed, given my chequered career during the first months of my postulancy. Great then was my amazement when, later that same week, Marie-Jeanne told me that the nuns were going to vote about me two weeks later.

The procedure for accepting a new novice is similar to that followed in deciding whether a novice should be allowed to make profession of vows. Neither decision rests solely with the candidate. The community will have to live with this person and it is only right that they should have a say in the decision. Marie-Jeanne explained to me what would happen. First, Véronique would ask me whether I was happy to go ahead, and if I agreed, she would then fix a date for the community to vote. (Decisions were always taken in a very democratic way in the community: whether it was the election of a new prioress or the acceptance of a new novice, every professed nun had a vote and was expected to use it.) On the day of the vote, the sisters would all assemble and I would formally ask to be accepted for my *prise d'habit*. Marie-Jeanne explained that this was more than a question of a simple request: the sisters would expect a brief résumé of my experience of the life so far together with the reasons why I wished to continue. She suggested that given the rather chaotic nature of the first half of my postulancy it might be a good idea to make some reference to the difficulties I had experienced during that time.

The great day arrived. Feeling as nervous as I had felt on the day I had first put on the white wig and stood up in court to say 'May it please your Lordship, I appear for the plaintiff', I entered the large parlour where all the professed nuns were assembled. Everybody smiled warmly at me, obviously anxious to put me at ease. They had all passed through this ordeal in their day. Still, I wondered about those smiles. Maybe they just wanted to show me that there were no hard feelings, before they voted to reject me ...

Getting a grip on my anxiety, I launched into the written speech I had prepared and which I had given to Marie-Jeanne in advance to censor. I told the sisters how difficult the first four months had been and, glancing up, I saw a few nods here and there. It hadn't gone unnoticed, then. I described how I had come to realise that the only way forward was by abandoning all resistance, by acknowledging my weakness and by trusting God to do what I was unable to do. As I declared all of this, it seemed so simple; I could not believe I would ever again make the same mistakes.

The nuns were persuaded. They voted to accept me for my *prise d'habit*. I had, of course, to leave the room while the beans were cast into the cup – a white bean for acceptance, a black bean for refusal. I don't know how many black beans there were, or indeed whether there were any at all. All I knew was that the final result was in my favour and Marie-Jeanne did not have to say one word when she came out to call me in again; her glowing face said it all. This was a victory for her as well as for me and I don't know which of us was happiest.

Chapter 16

A very busy time then began for Angèle and me. Angèle's *prise d'habit* was to take place on the last Sunday before Advent, the feast of Christ the King; mine was fixed for the feast of the Immaculate Conception, which fell on 8 December, two weeks later. Much had to be done by way of preparation. We had to be measured and fitted for our new habits by Solange, who, as well as looking after the garden, filled the office of wardrobe mistress. She was astonished at the differences in build between Angèle and me, in spite of the fact that we were the same height.

'But they are constructed completely differently!' she said to Marie-Jeanne during one of my fittings. 'This one has no shoulders at all!'

Then the liturgy had to be prepared for two separate ceremonies. Angèle and I chose the texts and the chants, Marie-Jeanne rehearsed the choir, while Véronique, who was an expert on the computer, although completely self-taught, prepared the booklets that would be used by the community and the congregation.

During this time, I went with Marie-Jeanne on one of her shopping expeditions in order to have my photograph taken for my French identity card. Except for my trip to hospital, I hadn't been outside the monastery for nine months. Now we were going to a large shopping centre, such as I had often frequented in pre-Aubépine times. I love shops. A wander around a shopping centre is a tranquillising and de-stressing experience for me always, so I was looking forward to this outing.

Marie-Jeanne parked the car in the car park and in we went.

As soon as we found ourselves amid the throngs of shoppers, I realised something was wrong. I didn't feel comfortable. Suddenly I realised how I looked – I who had always been so image-conscious and who had always dressed and made up carefully for a visit to town. Now my face was naked of make-up and my hair hadn't had a tint for almost a year. The roots had grown out and I felt I looked a sight. I looked around at the passing crowds. I didn't belong; I shouldn't be here. I wanted to run and hide myself somewhere, but Marie-Jeanne was speaking to me. She, of course, noticed nothing amiss.

'I'm going to do the community shopping,' she said. 'Will you just wander around and occupy yourself until I come back?'

I knew she did this from kindness. I thanked her, and she left me. What was I to do? I saw a coffee shop. One of my pleasures when shopping always had been to go and have a cup of coffee and a pastry. I brightened. I would go in there, have a coffee, feel normal again. And then it dawned on me: I had no money. I was a total misfit in this palace of consumerism; I had no home, no job, no money. I could not do so simple a thing as buy a cup of coffee. I sat down on a seat and stared straight ahead. It was as desolate a moment as any I have known.

Marie-Jeanne returned, we went and had my photo taken and set off for home again. I didn't say much on the way back. Marie-Jeanne asked me how I had enjoyed my day out and I replied that it had felt a little strange. She didn't press the matter. As we drove through the town, we passed an off-licence, its windows plastered with notices advertising the *nouveau Beaujolais*. I was suddenly struck to the heart by the realisation that never again could I buy a bottle of wine, never again relax with friends while sharing a glass of wine. I closed my eyes and thought of the God for whom I had abandoned all normal life. He made no sign. It was another bleak moment. Writing that night to my friend Sheelagh, I made light of it, but the bleakness breaks through: 'What I wouldn't give for a meal in a nice restaurant, with a bottle of good wine! (Or even medium wine. Oh heck! I'd settle for a bottle of plonk!)'

Angèle's big day came at last. She had spent the previous week in retreat in preparation and I envied her this time of solitude. The community had a little wooden hermitage (not unlike the tool sheds you can buy in any garden centre) at the edge of the woods and there the sisters went to make their individual annual retreats. It was furnished with a bed, a chair and a table. Now Angèle and I were going to have our first chance to live as hermits. I was dying to know how she got on.

Angèle loved snow. Before she began her retreat, she told us that her one wish was to have snow for the day of the ceremony. We laughed at her; the autumn had been a very mild one. But to everyone's astonishment, two days before the ceremony the skies darkened and the first flakes began to fall. By the feast of Christ the King, the snow lay so thick on the ground that there was some anxiety as to whether her family would be able to travel at all. Happily, they were, and she, her parents, her two sisters and her two brothers had a wonderful day. That evening in the refectory, I looked in amazement at this new Angèle, now formally known as Soeur Marie-Angèle du Coeur de Jésus. Gone was the young woman in jeans and tee shirt whose shiny hair was worn caught back in a scrunchie, and in her place was a tall young Carmelite in long brown robe and white veil, with only a little of that shiny hair showing in front. However, when she forgot about her flowing sleeves at the evening meal and one of them fell into her soup, it was the old Angèle who exclaimed, 'Oh, mince!'

A week later, it was my turn to go on retreat. Angèle's account of her stay in the hermitage had whetted my appetite, and my heart fell when Marie-Jeanne told me that there would be no question of staying there now that the weather had become so much colder. I would have to make my retreat in my cell.

Swallowing my disappointment, I tried to concentrate on the essence of the retreat, time alone with God to pray and reflect on the step I was about to take.

It was true that I found the cold difficult to bear. I was not Angèle; I was certainly not hoping for snow for the great day. In fact, as I told the sisters firmly, if I could really have my wish, I would ask for a day typical of the South of France in September: sunshine, blue skies and a temperature of about twenty-five degrees. I was no ascetic.

The night before the beginning of my retreat, I joined the community for night office for the last time as a postulant. The next time I was present for the night office in the chapel, I too would be dressed in the Carmelite habit. It was hard to believe. As we came out of the chapel after the office that night, I looked with a shiver at the frost already forming on the cloister windows. Then I noticed a number of the nuns whispering together and laughing. This was unusual, as it was the time of Great Silence, when nobody spoke. They were looking at me and pointing at the cloister windows. Puzzled, I looked at the clouded glass. Marie-Jeanne came over.

'That's not frost,' she hissed. 'It's condensation! The temperature is rising!'

Chapter 17

The temperature had indeed risen. And although it did not achieve anything like Mediterranean levels, by morning it was a very acceptable twelve degrees Celsius. I was delighted. This meant that, although not able actually to live in the hermitage, I would enjoy some pleasant woodland walks during my retreat.

My daily routine during the retreat began with an hour of prayer in my cell when I rose and a solitary recitation of the morning office. At eight, I joined the community for mass and, when it was over, went to the kitchen to collect the wicker basket which Claudine had packed with a flask of coffee, a small flask of hot milk and some bread, butter and jam. This I ate in solitude in my cell. The morning was divided between *lectio divina*, a meditative reading of the scriptures, work in the garden and another hour of prayer, taking me up to midday, when I recited the midday office and collected my lunch basket from the kitchen, taking a quick peek under the red and white checked napkin to see whether Claudine had left me one of her little treats: a bar of chocolate or a couple of her famous shortbread biscuits. I was rarely disappointed.

After lunch, I did some solitary choir practice. I sang alto in the choir and needed quite a bit of practice to familiarise myself with the many pieces of music in the nuns' extensive repertoire. Marie-Jeanne, ever anxious that her charges should improve the shining hour, suggested I bring the electronic keyboard from the novitiate to my cell, where I could practise away using the ear-phones without disturbing my neighbours. So it was that I sat at

the window of my cell every day from one until two rehearsing
silently the music that was to be used for the ceremony. It gave
an entirely new dimension to St John of the Cross, who spoke of
God as being like 'silent music'!

In the afternoon came a period of what we called 'spiritual
reading': reading a book on prayer or the spiritual life; another
hour of prayer, more work, a walk in the woods and a brief talk
with Marie-Jeanne, before the final hour of prayer, following
which I joined the community for vespers. After vespers, while
the community went to recreation, I collected the last basket of
the day from the kitchen, had my supper, said the office of vigils
and night prayer and went to bed early.

After two or three days of this regime, I felt this was the way
I wanted to live the rest of my life. The bliss of not having to
interact with the community was beyond belief. I knew I was
perfectly happy for the first time since my entrance; this happiness far outweighed what I had been feeling since July, it was
unalloyed. My daily meetings with Marie-Jeanne were serene
and productive – until the day that I decided to tell her how
content I was.

'So you're happy because you're alone, is that it?' she asked
me, after a moment's silence.

'Well, yes, in a nutshell, that's it,' I replied, and then, seeing
too late the trap I had set for myself, hastily added, 'but of course
I realise that one can't live the Carmelite life like this. It's a
community life after all, not an eremitical one.'

'Precisely,' Marie-Jeanne said drily. 'I wonder if the Lord is
trying to tell you something during your retreat.'

I felt paranoia claim me. Was she hinting at this late stage that
I shouldn't go ahead? Had she been thinking this all along?

'What?' I asked her. 'Are you saying that maybe I'm not
suited to the communal life? A retreat is just time out; I don't
expect it to be like this all the time. Besides, it's normal to enjoy
a bit of space and time to oneself.'

Marie-Jeanne smiled. 'I'm sure you're right,' she said. 'Don't worry about it unless it becomes an issue when you're back with the community again.'

This conversation nagged uneasily at the back of my mind for a while, but I forced myself to forget about it. Marie-Jeanne was right; it would be time enough to worry about it if it arose later on. I was sure it wouldn't. Well, I was fairly sure, anyway.

My two sisters and my brother were coming from Ireland for my *prise d'habit*. I was at once looking forward to this and apprehensive about it. What would they think of the place and of the community? They had always been supportive of the decision I had made – whether they understood it or not – but I hoped now that they would also feel happier about it. For one of my sisters, it would be the second visit, and I knew she had enjoyed the first.

The days passed quickly. After a few days of solitude and intensive periods of prayer (there were four each day) prayer seemed to become almost a habitual state of being. I had never experienced this before. It was as if this was the way we were meant to live, as if our natural state was to be in constant communion with this mysterious Entity, this Source of all life. Perhaps this was how it was in the original state of innocence, I thought, before whatever it was went wrong with the human race. I knew it couldn't continue, but while it did, I luxuriated in it.

> Let us rejoice, Beloved, and let us go to see ourselves in thy beauty,
> To the mountain or the hill where flows the pure water; let us enter further into the thicket.

As always, St John of the Cross had the words for it, I thought, reading this verse in his *Spiritual Canticle* one evening during the retreat. If I wondered what he meant by 'entering further into the thicket', I didn't dwell on it.

Chapter 18

That year, 8 December fell on a Sunday. Late on the Saturday afternoon, I left the monastery and headed towards the woods for the final walk of the retreat. It was a mild misty evening. A smell of wood smoke hung on the air and my happiness was tinged with a faint melancholy. I was beginning to feel homesick in advance for my retreat. It had been a period of unalloyed contentment and now it was about to end. I wondered about the step I was going to take. I had fallen in love with the Ineffable. The One I loved was unknown to me and I did not know where to find him. I had thought I would find him at Aubépine, but was I right? I had seemed to find him, or at least, traces of him, during my early visits, but where had he been since I entered? Not until this retreat had I managed to recapture something of the earlier experiences. And yet, I knew a little more about such things now: I knew that God was not necessarily in blissful feelings, and I knew that one could mistake the reflection for the reality. The most 'holy' feelings were, after all, only feelings. God was not there, it was necessary to move on, to travel further ...

> And all those that serve relate to me a thousand graces of
> thee,
> And all wound me the more. And something that they
> are stammering leaves me dying ...
> (St John of the Cross, *The Spiritual Canticle*)

While I was thinking about all these things, my steps had led me to the lower path in the wood where I had loved to go during that first visit to Aubépine. I headed for the cut-off tree stump, intending to sit there for a little. It was almost dusk. Suddenly, there was a commotion in the bushes to the right of the path, about fifteen yards ahead. I froze: perhaps it was a *sanglier* – a wild boar? Then, with the elegance of a ballerina, a deer leaped out onto the path before me and bounded down the hill to the left. While I still gazed after him, breathless with the joy of the vision, two more followed in rapid succession. A trinity of deer. And then I remembered the Song of Songs:

> The voice of my beloved!
> Look, he comes, leaping upon the mountains
> Bounding over the hills.
> My beloved is like a gazelle or a young stag.
> Look, there he stands behind our wall,
> Gazing in at the windows, looking through the lattice.
> My beloved speaks and says to me:
> 'Arise, my love, my fair one, and come away;
> for now the winter is past.'

That night after supper, Thérèse came to my cell armed with scissors and towels to cut my hair. She was the official cutter of hair in the community, and actually, although completely untrained in the art, she did it very well. My hair had been shoulder length when I had arrived at the Carmel, but it had grown much longer during the ten months that had passed and I had taken to wearing it tied back. Now Thérèse cut it short all over and, in spite of the grey roots, I really liked what I saw when I looked in the mirror. With a passing pang, I reflected that it was a pity I hadn't had it cut like that in the days when people could see it. Now it was going to be hidden by a veil for the rest of my life. Even as I made this reflection, I was appalled to see that something so banal would bother me at such a moment. Where were the fine feelings of that afternoon in the woods? Chastened,

I climbed into bed. I was reading when Marie-Jeanne knocked at the door to tell me that my family had arrived. She and Véronique had gone to the *hôtellerie* to welcome them and to explain that I was still on retreat, but that they would see me in the morning.

'They're all in great form,' she assured me as she left. 'Sleep well now.'

Before I fell asleep, I looked back in amazement over the past few years. From the moment of epiphany on the balcony in Luxembourg to the eve of my novitiate in Aubépine, what a journey I had made! I thought of my first visit to the Carmel and of my shock at the first sight of the community. Who would have thought that a little over two years later I would already have lived ten months with the community! As I lay there, I wondered: why me? Why did I react in that particular way to the words I read that night in Luxembourg? Who was God, that he could so powerfully draw someone like myself, someone far from mystical, someone who even tonight was momentarily more interested in the effect of a new hair style than in the events that were unfolding? I realised that I had been touched in so particular a way that night in Luxembourg that all my normal reactions and habits had been overridden by something beyond me, something that even now I did not understand and with which I was trying to co-operate, although haltingly, imperfectly and at times against my own will. I felt a sudden surge of love for this unknown and mysterious Lover, and then I slept.

The major events of the Aubépine phase of my life have, with one exception, taken place in winter and during the hours of darkness. I left my apartment in Luxembourg late on a January evening, I entered the monastery before dawn in the month of February, and I received the habit of a novice at seven on a December morning.

That morning, I was worried that my sisters and brothers

wouldn't wake in time after their long journey the previous day, but when I entered the chapel with Véronique at the end of the procession of nuns, there they were, Clare, Eileen and Liam, a rather forlorn little group huddled in the front pew, and my heart lifted to see them. I threw them a quick smile of reassurance and then followed Véronique to my place for the office of lauds, or morning prayer. I was already dressed in the brown robe and white veil of a novice, but wore no scapular, the long apron-like garment that Carmelites wear over the robe. Unlike the other nuns, neither was I wearing the great cream cloak, worn at mass and for certain parts of the office on solemn feasts. Today they were wearing it because of my *prise d'habit*.

The office of that day was full of meaning for me:

> The Lord has clothed me in the garments of salvation; he has wrapped me in the cloak of integrity ...

> Now, thus says the Lord, who created you, Jacob, who formed you, Israel: Do not be afraid for I have redeemed you; I have called you by your name, you are mine.

At the end of the office, Véronique left her place and went to a specially prepared chair beside the altar. I went and stood before her, while she asked me solemnly whether I wished to be received into the novitiate. In the prescribed words, I replied that I did. Then I knelt before her while Marie-Jeanne came to assist her in placing the scapular over my head and the cream cloak around my shoulders. Fully clothed now, I stood while Véronique greeted me for the first time by my new name – 'Desormais, tu seras appellée Soeur Noreen-Marie de Jésus' – and said a prayer of blessing; then I returned to my seat while she gave the exhortation. To my surprise, she delivered this in English, and I could only guess how long she must have spent in perfecting it. Then came the fraternal embrace, signifying my welcome into the community; as I went from nun to nun, each one whispered a few words of congratulation.

I spent most of that afternoon in the parlour with my sisters and brother. Just before the bell rang for prayer at 5 o'clock, Claudine came in with an enormous bouquet of flowers.

'This has just been delivered,' she said. 'It's for you, but I don't know who it's from.'

I opened the envelope that was pinned to the bouquet, and took out the card. 'With very best wishes from the Bar Council,' I read.

Suddenly I was back in the Law Library in Dublin. It seemed as though I had only slipped out for a moment, so vivid was my impression. There was my desk in the Irish Bay of the main library, right beside Dan Herbert's, with my briefcase lying half-propped against it as usual. I could see so clearly the papers and books that littered the top of the desk. I could hear Tommy the Crier calling the names of barristers over the intercom, according as solicitors asked for them at Reception. There was noise and bustle everywhere. People spoke urgently into telephones or stood in small groups, engaged in earnest discussion. Wigged and gowned barristers rushed past on their way to court. Across the Library, my friends were waving to indicate that they were on their way to the restaurant for coffee: Sheelagh O'Driscoll, Mary Flannery and Peter Somers, Seamus Sorohan, Olivia Meagher, Breda Ging, Twinkle Egan and many more; I couldn't believe I would never see them again.

'Who is it from?'

My sister Clare's voice pulled me back to the present. Dazed, I looked around the bleak, quiet little parlour and down at my new garments. I had exchanged a black robe for a brown and a white wig for a white veil. Perhaps in one way very little had changed. The life of a novice was, after all, not so very different from the life of a 'devil' – the name given to a barrister in his or her first year of practice. The novice has a mistress, the devil, a master. You could say, I reflected wryly, that the novitiate was 'devilling' without the alcoholic refreshment! I put the card from the Bar Council in the capacious pocket of my habit, and each time my fingers touched it my heart gave a curious little lurch.

Many old friends from my days in the Law Library wrote to me for the occasion: Anne Dunne, SC, Susan Denham, now a Supreme Court Judge, Kevin Waldron, former Director of Education at Kings Inns and, as I told Sheelagh when writing to her later, 'Niamh, Margo, Helen Ging, Helen Fanning, Bart Daly, Anne Confrey, Geraldine O'Connor – all the old and good friends.'

I was glad to know that I was still remembered in my old life.

Clare, Eileen and Liam stayed for three days. The weather continued to be dull and relatively mild until the morning of their departure, but that day we woke to find that the countryside had turned into a Christmas card overnight. Hoarfrost lay over everything. At first, we thought it was snow, so white did the landscape appear, but as the sun came out, the whole scene began to shimmer and sparkle, and we saw that every blade of grass, every leaf and twig, had its individual coating of ice.

I had seen hoarfrost once before in Aubépine. Then, I had walked in the woods through what seemed a cathedral of shining ice, where every tree was a towering white pillar. Suddenly, a hush had fallen on the woods and all creation seemed to hold its breath. I stood still, waiting. Then, with an unearthly tinkling sound the frost fell from every tree; all around my feet the forest floor turned white, while above, the cathedral disappeared like a vision, and the trees were just trees again. It was a moment of pure magic.

My family was enchanted with the landscape they saw from their windows, and I was happy that Aubépine had put on her best clothes for them before they left. They had not seen her in her hawthorn robe, but they had seen her winter ermine cloak. Until they left, a few hours later, she continued to shimmer and shine in the morning sun, like a queen arrayed in gold of Ophir

PART FOUR

'Negotiations and love songs are often mistaken for one and the same'

Paul Simon, *'Train in the distance'*

Chapter 19

About a week after my *prise d'habit*, the community began its annual retreat. Each nun made two long retreats every year: her private retreat, which she spent in the hermitage, in total seclusion from the rest of the community; and the community retreat. The form which a nun's private retreat took was up to her; it was essentially contemplative, and was regarded as time spent apart with God, to 'listen' to him in ever-deepening prayer. The community retreat, on the other hand, was a guided retreat. Typically, the guide was a priest – usually belonging to a religious order – who gave a series of talks on some particular theme appropriate to the monastic life, and who made himself available to the nuns for spiritual direction.

This was my first community retreat and I was looking forward to it. My anticipation dimmed a bit when I heard that the retreat master was a Jesuit. I knew no Jesuits, but I had a vague notion that they were intellectuals rather than mystics (as if the two were incompatible!), and I hoped we weren't going to have to spend eight days listening to what amounted to university lectures. My expectations therefore were not too high when we filed into the parlour on the evening before the retreat began to meet Père Lepoutre.

I don't know what I had expected, but it certainly wasn't a gaunt bearded man who would have looked more at home in the orange robes of a swami. I was immediately intrigued. Then he began to speak, and I was won over. He told us that the theme of the retreat was going to be the power of the Holy Spirit to heal and change our lives, This was what I most needed to hear and I went to bed that night feeling that the next week might be decisive for my whole novitiate and even for the rest of my life.

The following day, I knew this was indeed going to be something special. As if he had known what I had been living through, Père Lepoutre began by saying that we must start the retreat by a rereading of all that had happened to us during the past year, giving it a positive interpretation. This was a novel idea and I thought I would try it out. That night in bed, I began to think about the early months of my postulancy. They had been full of misunderstanding and unhappiness. What could I see in that that was positive? Père Lepoutre had suggested that in carrying out this exercise, we might meditate on the Burning Bush – a symbol for God in the Old Testament. God's love is like a fire, said Père Lepoutre, always new, always other.

I thought about this fire. I imagined it taking hold of me from the beginning of my postulancy. What does a fire do, when it begins to work upon anything? St John of the Cross describes the action of fire in his *Dark Night of the Soul*:

> for material fire, acting upon wood, first of all begins to dry it, by driving out its moisture and causing it to shed the water which it contained within itself.

The unconscious humour of this struck me as I thought about all the muffled tears I had shed during prayer in those early months. But smile as I might, I could not deny that this was indeed a 'drying-out' period in my life, when I felt emotionally drained and unable even to summon a smile at times.

> Then it makes it black, dark and unsightly, and even to give forth a bad odour …

Well, that certainly had happened. People had begun to see a very unpleasant side of me. I remembered Marie-Jeanne's comment about how I sometimes appeared arrogant, how the younger nuns were often intimidated by my attitude. I remembered the episode of the bell and another episode when I had strongly resented Thérèse's criticism of my punctuation when I was typing up a thesis for a customer. On that occasion I had announced to Marie-Jeanne that I had been the editor of a series of law reports in Ireland, and could therefore be presumed to know better than Thérèse how to punctuate. Marie-Jeanne had supported Thérèse and I had felt outraged. I had been vaguely aware at the time that I no longer seemed able to keep up the sort of appearances that one kept up in the world; it was as though my defences had been swept away and I was appearing as I really was. John of the Cross was quite right.

So what was the purpose of all this unmasking? What was the fire doing to the wood?

> ... as it dries it little by little, it brings out and drives away all the dark and unsightly accidents which are contrary to the nature of fire. And, finally, it begins to kindle it externally and give it heat, and at last transforms it into itself and makes it as beautiful as fire.

Yes, I could see now what was happening. This was the necessary preparation for the union with God for which I longed. All that pain had been the effect of the fire – the impact of God himself, of God's love – upon me and my life. It was not anything to regret, then, nor to be afraid of; on the contrary, it was something greatly to be desired.

So, had it worked? That was the next question, and the answer was perfectly obvious. It certainly had not. I was happier, it was true, but anyone with half an eye could see that there was still much in me that was 'black, dark and unsightly'. With this thought came a realisation that stopped me in my tracks: the bad days were not over. There would have to be much more burning before I could become one with the fire. I lay there, terrified. How could I bear it? My heart pounding, and every nerve in my body screaming 'No!' I tried to pray, But no words came. I picked up *Dark Night of the Soul* again, and rather desperately began to leaf through it, in the hope of finding something that would reassure me. But St John of the Cross is not the man to go to if you are in need of reassurance:

> We shall also learn from this comparison ... how true it is that after each of these periods of relief the soul suffers once again, more intensely and keenly than before. For, after ... the more outward imperfections of the soul have been purified, the fire of love once again attacks that which has yet to be consumed and purified more inwardly. The suffering of the soul now becomes more intimate, subtle and spiritual, in proportion as the fire refines away the finer, more intimate and more spiritual imperfections, and those which are most deeply rooted in its inmost parts. And it is here just as with the wood, upon which the fire, when it begins to penetrate it more deeply, acts with more force and vehemence in preparing its most inward part to possess it.

Reading this, I wished I could engrave it on my mind, so that I would always be aware in moments of anguish that it was the flame of love that was burning me. But I knew I would not. If I did, it would not be purification. It would be ecstasy.

Chapter 20

Christmas was upon us again. I had mixed feelings about it. It would be my first Christmas as a member of the community and I was looking forward to that. On the other hand, the social aspect of community life was greatly to the fore at Christmas and I was a little uneasy about how my new resolutions would stand up to it. I remembered from my *stage* the Christmas before that there was a whole week of festivities between Christmas and New Year and that it was the responsibility of those in the novitiate to devise a programme for the entertainment of the community. My memory of how this had panned out the previous year was that it had involved not a little stress in the life of the novitiate, but I had pushed away the uneasy feelings it had engendered in me at the time.

Christmas Eve and Christmas morning were beautiful. It had begun to snow a few days before, and when I walked through the cloisters on my way to midnight mass, the *préau* or cloister garden shone blue and white in the moonlight. The carols at mass were poignant and haunting and it was pleasant to have hot chocolate and biscuits in the warm refectory afterwards, with the fire lighting and talking allowed for once.

On Christmas morning, the nuns had a lie-in until 7 o'clock, but Marie-Jeanne, Angèle, Marie-Paule, Thérèse and I rose earlier for the traditional Christmas 'wake-up' call. On all other mornings of the year, the community was wakened by Véronique, who marched up and down the corridors at 5.45 ringing a little silver bell. How I hated the sound of that bell!

Véronique's cell was near mine and sometimes I woke a few minutes before she started her morning trip. Lying there drowsy and warm, I would hear her door open softly and every nerve in my body would tense in rebellion against the ringing which I knew would begin any moment. Up and down the corridors Véronique would go, the tinkling of her bell falling and rising. Outside the doors of the notoriously bad risers (such as myself) she would pause and shake her instrument of torture more loudly. It was usually necessary to open Marie-Paule's door and ring the bell inside to ensure that that young woman heard it. Marie-Paule was a very healthy sleeper. I used to lie there until the last stroke of the bell, hoarding every precious warm moment before my feet had to hit the cold floor and I tottered, half-conscious, to splash my face with cold water at the handbasin.

There was no hot water in the cells. How I longed, on the bitter mornings of the French winter, for my comfortable apartment in the Rue de Bourgogne, where the heating was timed to come on a half an hour before I got up and where I could go from the bed straight to a hot, perfumed shower, followed by a breakfast of freshly made milky coffee and toast! In Aubépine, I came downstairs shivering and half-awake, to drink a quick glass of black coffee before making my way to the chapel for morning prayer. Breakfast would not happen for another three hours.

But on Christmas morning, Véronique's little bell did not wake the community. Instead, the novitiate group, with Thérèse and Marie-Paule conscripted to swell its ranks, assembled with muffled giggles in the dark at the foot of the stairs: Angèle carried her flute, Marie-Paule had the guitar that I sometimes heard her playing in the woods on Sundays and feast days, Thérèse had her violin. I, not being able to play anything else, was armed with a tambourine. Marie-Jeanne gave the signal and we were off up the stairs, strumming, piping, singing:

> Il est né, le divin Enfant,
> Jouez hautbois, résonnez musettes!

Il est né, le divin Enfant
Chantons tous son évènement.

'The divine Child has been born, Oboes, play! Let us all sing of his coming!'

Up and down the corridors went our raucous choir and orchestra, those who were leading the way several beats ahead of those who brought up the rear, stumbling, giggling and dropping our instruments in the darkness. Marie-Jeanne's outraged musical sensibilities expressed themselves in hisses and whispered exhortations to slow down and keep together. But it was no use; we were having far too much fun. At each door, we upped the tempo until the occupant opened up and poked a tousled head out to applaud us. Some joined in the singing, all entered into the spirit of the thing. The wake-up call was one of the few things I enjoyed about that Christmas.

Chapter 21

The trouble began that afternoon in the novitiate. We were all tired. It had been a long night the night before and we had not had much sleep. At the afternoon recreation, neither Angèle nor I had much to contribute. Bleary-eyed, we sat around the battered novitiate table. Marie-Jeanne tried to rally us.

'You need to plan out the entertainment for the week,' she urged. 'Try to think of something different for each afternoon, something that the sisters might like.'

'But perhaps they mightn't like anything at all,' I knew I was being a party-pooper, but I couldn't stop myself, even when I saw Angèle glance at me, her large brown eyes anxious. 'Perhaps they might like to have some quiet time alone. Why should we foist all this entertainment on them?'

Marie-Jeanne looked at me over the top of her glasses. She knew where this was coming from.

'The sisters are not obliged to attend any of the events we arrange,' she said reprovingly. 'Some will come to one event and some to another. But they all look forward to this week. It's like a holiday for them. Our life is austere, but this brings a little relaxation.'

'Oh yes,' I said bitterly. 'They have a choice, but we don't have any. Not only have we to give up every afternoon to concerts or dramatic productions, but we have to spend the rest of our free time preparing them. This is Christmas, after all: I expected that Christmas in a monastery would be more spiritual. There's hardly time to pray, as far as I can see.'

Marie-Jeanne's lips tightened, and my heart sank. I knew that expression of old and I hadn't seen it since the feast of Our Lady of Mount Carmel. At the same moment, I felt the old familiar tightness in my chest and a stiffening of the muscles around my mouth. My face was freezing again; I couldn't smile at her. What sort of a place was this where a woman of my age couldn't express a contrary view without being treated like a recalcitrant schoolgirl? I turned to Angèle.

'Let's try to plan out our programme,' I said, my voice sounding strained to my own ears. I couldn't look at Marie-Jeanne and after a moment I heard the door closing quietly and knew that she had left the room. A sense of déjà-vu possessed me, together with a feeling that was almost dissociation. I had ruined everything. Angèle looked ill at ease. Once again, I felt alienated from the community. Why could I not enter into the spirit of the thing, like Angèle?

Somehow or other, we got through that afternoon and by the time the bell rang for prayer we had devised a programme for the week. The entertainments were to take place in the afternoons; the mornings were devoted to the normal routine. On St Stephen's Day, we planned to have a recital of CDs, chosen by us. On the following day, a community walk was arranged, followed by afternoon tea. Another day, there would be a concert, and on the final day the novices, aided by Marie-Paule, Thérèse and Marie-Jeanne, would present a play. I felt a weight of stress descend upon my heart. Where was the life of prayer I had come to find? It was all very well for Marie-Jeanne to say that the nuns needed some relaxation, but surely not a whole week of it? And what about the disruption this caused to the novices' spiritual life? Resentful and anxious, I went to the chapel for prayer knowing that the bad times were returning, and knowing too that this time matters would not be fixed by a simple chat with Marie-Jeanne in Kerith.

As always, prayer was a laying down of the load for an hour. I was in a place where I was understood even when I didn't understand myself. And as before, the relief produced tears. I begged for help to stop resisting, to be able to go with the flow, to be able to smile at Marie-Jeanne. If only all life could be prayer! It was so simple to be here, so simple to stop trying and just surrender in helplessness.

Next morning, I resolved to make a huge effort to enter into the spirit of the festivities. However, damage had been done the previous day; Marie-Jeanne was now convinced that I was going to resist whatever was proposed. As in the previous year, this triggered off uneasiness and self-consciousness in me. I felt I sounded falsely jolly during the various recreations, and by the end of each day I was emotionally drained. But in spite of it all, that deep place inside me still guarded its peace. I found it difficult to understand this, much less to explain it to anyone else, as is evident from a letter I wrote around that time to Sheelagh O'Driscoll:

> You ask me what it's like being a novice again, and whether I'm very happy. The answer to the second question is 'yes' , and to the first, it's like being given a second chance at life, with the hindsight I didn't have the first time, and with the help and constant accompaniment of people who really care how it works out – I mean the prioress, Véronique, and the novice mistress, Marie-Jeanne. At times it's exhilarating, like being on a roller-coaster, and at times terribly disconcerting ... The disconcerting bits are when you discover what you're really like, and when you have to try hard to swallow the home truths you hear from the novice mistress. But because you know they are told with great love and affection and a huge desire to remove all impediments to the continuing action of God, you learn bit by bit to accept them, after the initial feeling of having been thrown from a height. You will no doubt be glad to hear – you who often remarked upon it! – that my attitude of always being right has taken a great knocking!

The final day of that week was the worst. Strained and exhausted, I acted my part in the play, making a huge effort to appear to be enjoying myself. I thought I had succeeded, but this illusion was quickly dispelled by Véronique, who called me aside before the evening meal, which exceptionally was being held in the novitiate, where talking would be allowed.

'I understand from Marie-Jeanne that you don't enjoy any of this,' she said, 'but couldn't you at least make an effort to conceal that for the sake of the sisters?'

Speechless, I looked at her. There didn't seem to be anything I could say. However, she was waiting for a response, so I tried. I explained I had been trying, that I even thought I had been successful.

'No,' said Véronique. 'You aren't really trying. You haven't yet surrendered your own feelings and wishes to God. Real humility and surrender go hand in hand. I thought you had surrendered last July, but here you are again, back in the old rut. At least try to make some effort for the rest of the evening.'

She turned away, leaving me in a state approaching despair. I went in to the novitiate, wondering how I could make a greater effort than that which I had been making all afternoon. I felt at the end of my resources and conscious now that not only Marie-Jeanne but also Véronique would be watching me. The novitiate was full of noise and merriment. Crackers were being pulled, riddles and jokes being read out. I sat down and looked for someone to pull a cracker with. There must be very little that is more difficult to do than to act as if you are enjoying yourself when you have just been instructed to do so and those who have instructed you are watching. It was an evening of misery, but even the worst evenings come to an end, and at last I was able to regain the sanctuary of my silent cell.

I sat there for a long time before I went to bed, wondering what was happening to me. I did not feel that I belonged here. Somehow, in all that was most essential to me, the nuns and I were not on the same wavelength. During the months that had passed since the conversation with Marie-Jeanne in July, I had had what now seemed to me to be a false sense of belonging, bolstered up by all the excitement of the preparations for my *prise d'habit*.

What was wrong? Were the differences between the nuns and me cultural? Certainly there were language problems; I could not always express myself as clearly as I wished. And yet I knew it was something deeper than that; on my journey in search of God, the path where I felt most content was a solitary one. In Aubépine, one travelled always with others. Yet everything had seemed to lead me there. Was I looking for the wrong path? Should I try to adapt my desires?

Or should I leave Aubépine?

Even as that last question formulated itself in my mind, I rejected it vehemently. Where could I go if I left Aubépine? Where else could I continue the quest? How otherwise could I lead a life of total prayer and contemplation? Returning to 'the world', to the life of a lawyer, was unthinkable. No, I could never leave Aubépine.

Chapter 22

One morning in January 1997, Véronique assembled the community for a special meeting. This did not often occur, but when it did, it was a matter of some excitement. We all filed in to the large parlour where such meetings were usually held and, although the rule of silence precluded the sort of chattering that would obtain at any assembly of this kind in the world outside, an electric air of anticipation hung over the room. Véronique began by reminding us that we had a rule of strict enclosure, and that although the traditional symbols of enclosure such as grilles and high walls had not existed for many years, it was nevertheless neither desirable nor appropriate that persons who were not members of the community should be able to go anywhere they wished within the community property.

I began to see where this was leading. The community owned several acres of land surrounding the monastery and this included some woodland. Part of the property was always regarded as being 'within the enclosure' and therefore accessible only by the nuns, while the rest was open to visitors to the monastery, who could thus avail themselves of pleasant walks in the woods while they were staying at the *hôtellerie*. However, the separation between the enclosure and the external part of the land was marked only by a low wire fence and quite frequently people climbed over this, either not recognising or not caring that it indicated a boundary.

Indeed, as a visitor to the Carmel, I had once made this mistake myself. During the ten days I had spent there in the summer of 1994, I had become friendly with another guest, Gérard, a

widower in his fifties. He was a great walker and knew most of
the trails in the area around the monastery. He occasionally
invited me to go with him – indeed it was he who had shown me
the walk which led to the viewing-point with the tree-trunk.
One day, we set off through the woods to hunt for the wild
strawberries that grow in abundance around Aubépine. As we
wandered along a little woodland track, filling our handkerchiefs
with the tiny ruby-like fruits, we came to a thin wire stretched
across the path at waist level.

'I don't know why this is here,' said Gérard. 'All this land
belongs to the nuns, so there is no danger that we will be
trespassing if we cross it.'

We climbed over the wire and wandered on. The woods were
thinning out a little ahead of us and suddenly we came to an
open space. We looked around, puzzled. The place looked culti-
vated. There was a sudden movement and a nun stepped out
from behind a tree about a hundred yards away. It was Thérèse.

'Mon Dieu!' exclaimed Gérard, horrified, 'We're in the nuns'
garden!'

And so saying, he turned and fled; me hot on his heels,
unsure what the penalty might be for breaking into the nuns'
enclosure. I felt very embarrassed that evening at supper when
Thérèse brought in the tea-trolley, but to my great relief she
never mentioned the escapade.

Other, more serious trespasses occurred from time to time,
and their frequency increased as the countryside in the region of
Aubépine became more built-up. I had had a surreal experience
in the garden one peaceful evening the previous September. I
was sitting under a tree reading when I heard loud voices
coming from the woods.

'Left, right, left, right, AND right turn ...'

I looked up from my book in time to see a platoon of soldiers
in camouflage, rifles on their shoulders, emerge from the wood
and march across the lawn in front of me. Staring in disbelief, I
watched them disappear around the side of the house and march

away down the drive, their chanting fading into the distance.

This then was the background to the community meeting and Véronique was now proposing to us that we build an enclosure fence all around the property. Marie-Paule, with her usual practicality, asked what this would involve. Véronique had made enquiries and told us that first of all, the woodland and undergrowth would have to be cleared all around the perimeter. Next, holes for the posts would have to be drilled, the posts themselves inserted and the holes filled with cement. Then the sections of steel wire fence would have to be fitted between the posts. The task would be a very lengthy one – Véronique could not envisage it taking less than six months – but more importantly, it would be extremely costly to have all this work carried out by contractors. Therefore – and now she was coming to the really important part – how would we feel about doing some of it ourselves? In a nutshell, what she was proposing was that we cleared the woodland, with any help we could get from friends of the community. Following that, workmen would drill the holes and finally we would erect the fencing ourselves.

There was a moment's silence when Véronique had finished speaking, then an excited babble of conversation broke out. All the younger nuns were enthusiastic; the older ones were more cautious.

'You'll kill yourselves,' said Marie-Cécile from her wheelchair, her lined old face anxious. 'That sort of thing is men's work!'

The younger ones laughed at her.

'We're strong,' said Marie-Paule confidently, her eyes sparkling. 'We're well used to clearing woodland. We do it all the time.' Clearly she relished the task, and would be in her element, constructing something in the woods she loved.

As I listened to all of this, I could feel my heart sinking. My mind leaped ahead and I could see months and months of communal work where everybody pulled together in a jolly hockey-sticks sort of a way, while the regular rhythm of prayer and silent work fell by the wayside. I said nothing, but turned inwardly to the One I had come here for and tried to hand it all over to him.

> *Don't let me follow my own inclinations here, because I no longer know what is best for me. Maybe You brought me here precisely in order to turn my whole life upside down; to find only action where I had looked for contemplation ... But I know You are with me, even if I walk in the Valley of Darkness.*

Before we left the meeting that day, the community had decided to put Véronique's plan into action. However, we had a short respite: we would not begin until the springtime. It was therefore fixed that we would begin in mid-April, after Easter.

I left the parlour with my heart full of foreboding.

Chapter 23

Lent came again – my second Lent in Carmel. It was no better than the previous one; I seemed to be stumbling from one disaster to another. Although in themselves they were small and even petty things, in my hypersensitive state they assumed huge and painful proportions. Some of them were misunderstandings, but even while I resented this, I could see that they had arisen because my behaviour was so often genuinely open to criticism.

For example, there was the re-allocation of Marie-Paule's duties while she was temporarily away helping out another Carmel. I was unaware until shortly before her departure that some of the other nuns had taken over her jobs. Angèle seemed particularly burdened, having now to do the laundry and the ironing as well as all her own jobs. I hadn't been asked to do anything, and it suddenly occurred to me that perhaps I ought to have offered. Well, it wasn't too late, so I went to Marie-Jeanne and asked if there was anything I could do to help.

'No, don't worry about it', said Marie-Jeanne, 'everything has been taken care of.'

Her attitude seemed a bit dismissive, and I was surprised.

'Yes, I know,' I replied, 'but I thought that perhaps I could help one of those who have taken on extra duties. For example, Angèle has a lot on her plate, so I thought that maybe I could do the ironing?'

To my astonishment, Marie-Jeanne's expressive face took on that tight-lipped appearance which habitually greeted my more rebellious or critical utterances.

105

'No thank you,' she said. 'As I've just told you, it has all been taken care of.'

And she turned away.

Of course, I should have left it alone, but I didn't. Stung by her attitude, which I didn't understand, I told her that I was only trying to help, my own voice to my dismay taking on the strained and querulous tone that this sort of interaction with her always produced.

She turned back, her face flushed.

'You are not trying to help; you are trying to impose your own will and criticise what has already been done. Just leave it alone, please.'

Smarting with injustice and biting my tongue I left her. Of course I couldn't get it out of my head for the rest of the day. It followed me to prayer, where in the silence and the peace of that time and place it completely took over my mind. Try as I might to hand it over, back it came again like a tennis ball neatly returned over the net. Why had she reacted like that? I painstakingly scrutinised my own motives; I was as sure as I could be that there had been no trace of what she had accused me of. I knew that this time I had genuinely wished to take my part, and had felt that I should offer, since I had not been asked. Round and round it went and I was unable to stop even though I knew how ridiculous it was. One thing that I was certainly learning in all of this was my own helplessness, and somewhere deep down I knew that was a good thing. The masks were falling, bit by bit.

One evening a few days later, I was watering the flowers in the *préau* after compline. It was the time of the Great Silence, when talking was prohibited unless absolutely necessary: consequently, it was a time when I was relaxed and at peace because I knew that nothing more could befall me until the next day.

I was wrong.

As I stood mindlessly watching the soothing jet of water playing over the flowerbeds, I heard a movement behind me. Startled, I swung around. It was Véronique, gesturing to me to avoid playing the hose on some tender young plants that were just beginning to sprout. Nodding to show that I had understood, I returned to my watering and thought no more about it.

Next day I went to have my monthly meeting with Véronique. Each nun met with the prioress once a month for about an hour. It was an opportunity for mutual discussion and a chance for the nuns to get spiritual direction, if that was their wish. I always enjoyed these meetings, and looked forward to my turn every month. This occasion was no different and after the usual preliminaries, Véronique asked me how I was getting on. I admitted that I was going through a difficult time and that the old stresses were making themselves felt again. She looked concerned.

'Yes,' she said, 'I suspected something of that sort was happening when I heard about your demand to take over the ironing.'

Considerably taken aback, I began to explain that on that particular occasion I had been misunderstood.

'Oh, no,' said Veronique firmly. 'It was quite clear to Marie-Jeanne that you were annoyed at not having been asked to do anything, and you wanted to let it be known. I saw the same sort of thing yesterday in the way you reacted when I asked you to be careful of the small plants. You looked outraged.'

'Outraged? My goodness, no!' I laughed at the thought. 'No, I was just startled – my mind was miles away at the time.'

'It was perfectly clear to me that you deeply resented my telling you what to do. As always, you knew better than anyone else.'

To my dismay, I felt weak tears filling my eyes. I felt completely helpless. It seemed that no matter what I said, Véronique was going to cling to her belief. For a moment wild thoughts filled my mind of the sort of tests nuns underwent in sixteenth-century monasteries. Perhaps Véronique was just testing my humility or obedience? But even as the thought passed through my mind I knew it was ridiculous. Véronique was a twentieth-century woman and that sort of medieval behaviour was not at all her style. If she was persisting in her view, it was because she genuinely believed it to be true.

The next event, however, was very different. There was no misunderstanding at all on this occasion. Towards mid-March, two friends, Anne and Geraldine, had come to visit me from Dublin. They had spent two days in the nearby town, coming out each afternoon by taxi to the Carmel. It had been a wonderful interlude in a dark period, during which I felt I had come back to life again. Strangely, the contrast between how I felt when I was with them and how I felt when I was with the community still didn't cause me to question my life in Aubépine.

They brought me a present of a book about Dublin. That night, after they had left, I sat in my cell turning over its pages. It was full of wonderful photographs. Grafton Street: people standing outside Bewley's, in groups and alone. I would never wait there again to meet a friend for coffee. O'Connell Street: Eason's. I would never again push open those glass doors and inhale the delicious smell of new books, never browse the stands where the latest releases were displayed, never enjoy the titillating pleasure of searching for a third book to make up a 'three for two' offer. My eyes filled with tears again. Suddenly, I wanted so much to be in Dublin.

The next day was Sunday. It was the eve of St Patrick's Day and at first the mood of homesickness was still upon me. As the day wore on, however, I began to feel better. In part, this was because Sundays seemed generally to provide me with a respite from the constant struggle. The extra times of prayer were times of rest when I entered another dimension, a deeper part of my being where there was constant peace even in the height of battle. During prayer, I seemed to descend there – or perhaps it rose up and enveloped me. The fact that there were more opportunities to be alone also helped; I was becoming increasingly aware that I revived in solitude.

On Sundays, we got up at 6.45, an hour later than usual. This meant that instead of starting the day with an hour's prayer, we began with the office of lauds. The morning hour of silent prayer could be made alone at any time we liked. It was this, together with the fact that there were no classes in the novitiate, that gave me my much-needed solitude.

It was a lovely spring day, warm in a way that would have been very unusual for March in Ireland. I set off after lunch for a walk in the woods, carrying a book, pleasurably anticipating a quiet time on the tree-stump with the view. As I approached the glass door into the garden, I was surprised to hear voices coming from the nearby staircase. Then Marie-Jeanne's unmistakeable and irrepressible laugh rang out. I stood and waited, curious to see the explanation for this unusual breach of the rule of silence. For a few moments, nothing was visible, but more muffled laughter and intriguing bumps came from higher up, around the bend of the staircase. Then Marie-Jeanne appeared, descending backwards, arms spread wide. She was followed by Angèle and Marie-Paule struggling with one end of a small iron bedstead, which appeared to be pushing them down the staircase. The other end was held by Véronique and Thérèse, who were clearly having some difficulty controlling matters. Everybody seemed to be having a lot of fun.

They didn't see me. I stood there in the shelter of a doorway and watched the proceedings. All the younger members of the community were there, together with Véronique and Marie-Jeanne. I was the only one who had been left out. A dark mist filled my brain. I wanted to yell and scream at them. I wanted to lie on the floor like a small child and throw a tantrum. I was ten years old again, sitting in the back row at school during choir practice, listening to the whispers of three girls I had thought were my friends. Heads together, they were planning a picnic at the weekend. 'But don't tell Noreen Mackey,' said one of them; 'she'll want to come too.' They didn't know that I could hear them, and I wept with all the agony and despair that a child feels when excluded from an inner circle.

But now I didn't weep, although the emotions I experienced

were identical to those felt by my 10-year-old self. Using all my will power, I forced myself to turn away and walk through the glass door into the garden. Outside, I stood still. Everything in me wanted to go back to let them know that I knew they had left me out. I knew I was being ridiculous, but the battle was real. I tried to turn to God and I begged him to help me. It seemed to me that I had reached a decisive moment: if I was serious about the life I was trying to live, I would now walk down to the woods, hand over the hurt to God and get on with things. I walked towards the woods. Yes! I would do it! Suddenly my heart started to sing. Thank you God! You are helping me to do something that was absolutely impossible for me! I walked on, I turned around, I was walking back towards the garden door. Don't, don't, I pleaded with myself. Don't go back. God will help you. Go back to the woods. But I carried on towards the door; now I was pushing it open, I was advancing across the hallway, towards the stairs. The hallway was deserted, but voices from above, together with the iron bedstead and other bric-a-brac in the hall bore witness to the ongoing work. Deaf now to every inner voice and almost on automatic pilot, I started to climb the stairs. There they were, all of them, around the first bend, struggling with another bed, laughing and enjoying themselves together.

'Can I help?' I asked loudly, my voice echoing strangely in my own ears.

Five startled faces turned towards me.

'No, we're fine thanks,' said Véronique, smiling, but Marie-Jeanne, seeing my thunderous expression, realised that this was something more than a polite offer and came down towards me anxiously, ushering me back towards the hall.

'What on earth is this about?' she asked quietly.

'I simply want to know if I can help, that's all.'

'We're fine,' said Marie-Jeanne, 'we were just bringing down some old beds from the attic, but everything is almost done now. But thanks anyway. Were you off for a walk?'

I stared at her. I was now beyond all reasoning.

'It doesn't look to me as if you've finished,' I said, and brushing past her rudely I mounted the stairs and accosted Marie-Paule, who was at the receiving end of the second iron bed.

'I'll take that!' I said, almost thrusting her aside.

Astonished, she let go and moved out of my way. I was conscious of five pairs of eyes upon me. All the laughter stopped. Down we went, with me clinging grimly to my corner of the bed. We reached the hall in total silence and set down the bed. Everyone stood there uneasily. My fury increased. So they only enjoyed themselves when I wasn't there!

'Is there any more?' I demanded.

Véronique found her voice.

'No,' she said. 'There isn't any more. Thanks for your help.'

I turned away. Marie-Jeanne was standing where I had left her, her face expressionless. Marching past her, I made my way back to the garden door, a strange dizziness in my head and a ringing in my ears. I was vaguely aware of having crossed a boundary, but it seemed very important not to allow myself to think about it just then. Treading carefully, I opened the door and went out to the garden for the second time. Less than ten minutes had passed since I had last been there, but it seemed a lifetime.

The sun was still shining, the birds were chirping away as before. I stood there, dazed. What had I done? My head was still spinning and my heart was racing. My anger had not died down, but added to it now was a sense of total humiliation. I had made a complete fool of myself. Hardly knowing what I was doing, I went on down the path towards the woods and sat on the tree-trunk. There I forced myself to face reality. I had thrown a tantrum. Everyone present had seen it. What was I doing in this place, this way of life? It was for selfless people; how could I ever live it? Far from becoming selfless, I was regressing into the selfishness of childhood. For a long time I sat there trembling, trying before God to face the fact of my own egoism, trying to believe that he still loved me, in spite of my awfulness.

Chapter 24

'*Le Jour des Anciens Lits*' — the Day of the Old Beds, as Véronique began to call it in an effort to make me feel less terrible about it, proved to be another turning point. Both she and Marie-Jeanne could not have been kinder in their interpretation of my behaviour. Heaping coals of fire upon my head, they explained to me that the thing had not been organised at all; Véronique, Marie-Paule and Thérèse had been struggling down the stairs with one of the beds when Marie-Jeanne and Angèle had happened to pass. Gratefully, the others had conscripted them to the task. For my own part, my contrition was total. I recognised too that in some way I barely grasped, it had been a good thing. By now I knew how essential it was that the false self should be unmasked, so that one could stand in truth before the living God. I was nowhere near that place, but every step that helped in the unmasking was to be welcomed, no matter how painful.

> *I have discovered a new sort of joy: that of experiencing Your work of destruction in me. It is painful, but I can describe it as a joy because anything that brings me nearer to You is utter happiness. You are destroying me in this way because You want to unite me with Yourself. And I understand that it is the old 'me' that is being destroyed, the false self that I have spent all my life fabricating. When this is dead, the true 'me', the child of God, will be able to live fully.*

A newly peaceful period commenced. Once again, St John of the Cross's map of the route showed the road that I was following:

112

The purgative process allows intervals of relief, wherein, by the dispensation of God, this dark contemplation ceases to assail the soul in the form and manner of purgation, and assails it after an illuminative and loving manner, wherein the soul, like one that has gone forth from this dungeon and imprisonment, and is brought into the recreation of spaciousness and liberty, feels and experiences great sweetness of peace and loving friendship with God, together with a ready abundance of spiritual communication. This is to the soul a sign of the health which is being wrought within it by the said purgation and a foretaste of the abundance for which it hopes. (*Dark Night of the Soul*)

So it was with me. A new humility coloured both my prayer and my relationship with the community. I realised that I had nothing to recommend me to God, but that he had always known this, even if I hadn't, and he had called me nevertheless. There was something profoundly liberating about being able to look at oneself and say, 'It doesn't matter that I'm envious, selfish and petulant. God knows all this and loves me anyway. It makes no difference to him.' There was liberation too − although it was painful − in the fact that the community saw me as I was. No need now to keep up any appearances; there were none to keep up. The energy that had gone into that could now be directed to the ongoing struggles of the journey.

Work on the enclosure fence began shortly after Easter. In my new frame of mind, it didn't at first seem as dreadful as I had anticipated it would be. The day we began was blue and gold; a perfect April day with just enough coolness in the morning air to set the blood tingling. It was a good day for starting anything. After a more substantial breakfast than usual, the work crew, comprising Marie-Jeanne, Marie-Paule, Thérèse, Angèle and me, set off for the Prairie, which was to be our starting-point. We departed cheering and in fine style, Marie-Paule driving the community tractor, Samson, with the rest of us crowded into a small cart towed behind. Claudine and some of those who were staying behind came to wave us off at the top of the drive and there was a holiday atmosphere about it all. We were a motley crew, dressed in jeans and tee shirts, with an eclectic variety of headgear to protect us from the sun. Angèle had her usual wide-brimmed sombrero, which gave her, as one of the old nuns said, a certain *allure*; Therese's dark curls peeped out from under a bright red linen cap; Marie-Paule's denim baseball cap was jauntily turned back to front, and I had a bright green cotton sunhat that Marie-Jeanne had given me on my first St Patrick's Day in the monastery, in honour of Ireland. Marie-Jeanne herself looked like a gypsy, with a cotton scarf around her head tied in a knot at the nape of her neck and Marie-Paule teased her that she had forgotten her hooped earrings. My spirits rose; I began to wonder what I had been afraid of.

At the top of the sharp descent to the Prairie, we unloaded our tools: long secateurs, heavy scythes, chain saws and other machinery used in clearing woodland. Our aim was to start clearing away the heavy undergrowth and small saplings along the line that marked the location of the proposed fence. The plan was that according as an area was cleared, part of the fence would be erected, and we would then move on to the next area. Getting the heavy and dangerous tools down the overgrown descent was our first challenge and required some teamwork. Marie-Jeanne was our overseer, and eventually, with some difficulty, the task was accomplished. We then set to at the bottom of the hill. I, as a person not noted for physical dexterity, was not allowed near chain saws or other potentially lethal machinery, Marie-Jeanne explaining firmly that she wished to return us all to the monastery at midday with a full complement of arms and legs However, she was happy to let me attack the lighter undergrowth with secateurs, a task that proved to be much more strenuous than it appeared.

We worked without a break from 9 o'clock. At about 10.45, as I was bending my aching back to the task for what seemed like the thousandth time, I heard a faint *'coucou!'* coming from above, and looked up to see Véronique clambering down the track from the road with a large basket.

'Pause café!' she called.

Instantly, we all downed tools. The screaming noise of the heavy machinery stopped and a blissful silence fell over the field as we made our way to the shade of the clump of trees where Véronique was starting to unpack her basket. Throwing myself gratefully onto the ground, I watched as she unloaded ice-cold bottles of water beaded with droplets, flasks of coffee, bars of chocolate, apples and plastic containers full of Claudine's short-bread cookies. Chatter broke out as we cooled down and began to enjoy the impromptu picnic. I looked around at these women who had become my sisters: Angèle was propped against the trunk of a large oak crunching a large apple, her short fair hair falling in damp tendrils from under the straw hat, her face and arms bronzed from a year and a half of outdoor work, a look of utter contentment on her face; Marie-Paule was flat on her back, as completely relaxed as a cat, a bottle of water tilted towards her mouth. Even I felt at ease and I wondered whether I was changing at last.

Chapter 25

A few days later, Marie-Jeanne arrrived at recreation in the
novitiate with a beaming face.

'I have some news for you two,' she announced, 'and you are
really going to love it! Guess where we are going to celebrate
your birthdays this year?'

Angèle and I both had birthdays in May, one day after the
other. We were intrigued by Marie-Jeanne's announcement.
Where else would we spend our birthdays but at Aubépine? But
we were wrong.

'This year', Marie-Jeanne said impressively, 'we are going to
celebrate your birthdays in Lisieux!'

Lisieux! To a Carmelite, Lisieux is as Mecca is to a Muslim.
One of the greatest saints of Carmel had lived and died there. S
Thérèse of the Child Jesus, sometimes known as the Little Flower
entered the Carmel of Lisieux in 1888 at the age of fifteen and
died there of tuberculosis nine years later. This year was the
centenary year of her death and, as Marie-Jeanne went on to
explain to us, it had been decided to hold a five-day conference
at Lisieux for all the Carmelite novices of France. We were wildly
excited. The excitement was on two levels: a visit to Lisieux was
in itself a wonderful event, but a visit anywhere was an extra
ordinary happening for an enclosed nun. That night in bed
reflected on the enormous change that had occurred in my life
over the past year. I, who had travelled at a whim anywhere in
Europe and thought nothing of deciding on a Friday morning to
catch the 5 o'clock train from Luxembourg in order to spend the
weekend in Paris, was now in a state of excitement bordering or

the infantile at the prospect of spending a few days in a provincial town in Normandy with a group of nuns!

As the time for the trip drew near, we began to make preparations. Marie-Jeanne's friend Yvette was going to take a few days' leave and drive us to Lisieux. She would then take the opportunity of doing a bit of sight-seeing in Normandy while we were at *les sessions des jeunes*.

Les sessions des jeunes! I didn't know whether I was amused or annoyed by the fact that the conference was called 'sessions for young people', implying as it did that all novices were young. I knew for a fact that they were not: apart from myself, there was Clothilde in a Carmel in the Paris province, whom I had met during my first *stage*: she was fifty years old. And I knew there were others too; not many, it was true, but enough to make the description of the sessions inaccurate. What concerned me about the description was that it seemed to give expression to an almost subconscious belief that novices were never middle-aged and I had occasionally felt that it was this assumption that made it so difficult for Marie-Jeanne and I to relate to each other. She had no terms of reference for being novice mistress to a 48-year-old novice. But then, I reflected wryly, my behaviour was not calculated to disabuse her of the notion that novices were like children.

To prepare us for the *sessions*, Marie-Jeanne asked Claudine to give us a short course in the novitiate on the writings and spirituality of St Thérèse. This was a great pleasure for me, as St Thérèse had been a friend from my teenage years.

Thérèse Martin was born in Alençon in 1873, the spoiled youngest of five girls in a deeply Christian family. Her mother's death when Thérèse was three had a profound effect on her, and plunged her into neurosis. From a happy, outgoing child, she became nervous and withdrawn. Following the family's move to Lisieux, she clung to her two eldest sisters, Marie and Pauline, and she broke down completely when Pauline, who she regarded as her second mother, became a Carmelite nun. Her illness lasted some months, and there was fear that she might die. Her father and sisters, full of faith, prayed for her, and she herself, as she relates in her autobiography, *The Story of a Soul*, had a spiritual experience in which she realised that Mary the mother of Jesus loved her like her own child. Whatever the truth of what the 9-year-old child experienced, she recovered from her illness and picked up again the threads of the life of a middle-class child in nineteenth-century France.

Influenced, no doubt, by the example of her sister Pauline, and subsequently by Marie who also entered Carmel, Thérèse began, around the age of eleven, to say that she too would be a Carmelite. Her elders were amused, but she was adamant. Overcoming all resistance, she joined the Carmel of Lisieux at the age of fifteen and lived there until her early death at twenty-four. Some years later, Catholic France was riveted by the publication of her autobiography, a short book written at the request of Marie and Pauline during her final illness. This book, ostensibly an account of her childhood and early days in the monastery, revealed an extraordinary life of faith and, above all, a trust in God that knew no bounds. For Thérèse, God was a loving father, who drew good even from the faults of his children, and who would forgive them anything, if only they turned to him. She took the parable of the Prodigal Son literally, as indeed Jesus meant it to be taken. In a France where traces of Jansenism still infected the practice of religion, the book was revolutionary and spread like wildfire. Soon it was being translated into almost every language and, in record time and during the lifetime of her sisters, Thérèse was canonised a saint.

I had always loved her. There was something so appealing about a saint who had struggled with neurosis. I had visited Lisieux a couple of times when I lived in Luxembourg, but this visit was going to be different. To go there as a Carmelite! It was unbelievable. We would not, of course, stay at the Carmel where she had lived. Fifty novices would be assembled for the *sessions* and there was no way that the Carmel could accommodate ever a quarter of that number. So, as Marie-Jeanne explained, we would stay at *l'Hermitage*, a retreat and conference centre built at Lisieux to help cope with the thousands of pilgrims who flocked there every year.

Claudine's talks in the novitiate whetted our appetites even more. Pleased to see our enthusiasm, Marie-Jeanne began to think of ways of making the trip even more memorable.

'Maybe we could visit Alençon en route,' she suggested one day in the novitiate.

This was even better. Neither Angèle nor I had ever been to Alençon.

With the prospect of the journey before me, the cloistered atmosphere of the Carmel did not press so greatly upon me. I was looking forward too to meeting novices from other Carmels, especially those who were nearer my own age. It would be interesting, I thought, to talk to them, and to find out whether their experiences were similar to my own. Our work on the enclosure fence had temporarily stopped, in order to allow workmen to drill holes for the posts along the half-mile or so that we had cleared so far, and I was happy to have recovered the normal rhythm of work and prayer. All was well in my life for the moment.

Chapter 26

The time seemed to pass very slowly, but eventually May arrived and we were down to the last-minute details in our planning. Packing was a very different experience from what it had been in pre-Aubépine days. Now everything I needed to bring for the five days fitted into a bag so small that it would not have done for a weekend away in the past. There were no cosmetics to pack, no bulky accessories. Just a couple of clean veils, changes of underwear and books. How simple life could be! Why, I wondered, had I always made it so complicated?

Marie-Jeanne was anxious to avoid long delays in traffic, so we were going to set out at the crack of dawn. We were to be in the refectory for an early breakfast, she instructed us, at 4 a.m. and to be ready to leave at 4.30. Leave at 4.30! Was she serious? Beating the traffic was one thing, but surely this was taking matters to extremes? My remonstrations were of no use. We were starting out at 4.30, and that was that.

It was, therefore, a bleary-eyed Marie-Jeanne and I who met in the pre-dawn refectory one morning in late May. We had crept like mice down the dark stairs so as not to disturb the still peacefully sleeping community. In the refectory, we found that Claudine had left flasks of coffee and hot milk for us, and bread rolls wrapped in cloths to keep them fresh overnight. We sat down. But where was Angèle? This was very unusual. Angèle, as I had good reason to know, was always first out of bed in the mornings. Day after day, I would grit my teeth as her feet thudded to the floor two cells away at the first sound of Véronique's terrible little bell. How did she do it? Didn't she ever feel like seizing just one minute more in bed? My competitive nature triggered by this self-abnegation, I had on a number of occasions fallen out of bed myself the moment the bell began and raced through the morning ablutions in a vain attempt to get downstairs before her. But it was never any good; when, breathless and dishevelled, I reached the chapel, there she knelt, straight-backed and composed, looking for all the world as if she had been there all night. I couldn't work out how she did it, and it irritated me beyond measure. So now I sat in the refectory smugly as Marie-Jeanne fumed. Finally Angèle rushed in, veil crookedly pinned, for once looking the way I felt every morning. I hoped she noticed how composed I was, sitting there sipping my coffee and finishing my roll.

But pettiness of this nature was soon put aside as we heard a car roll up to the door of the *hôtellerie*. Yvette had arrived, and the adventure was about to begin. I felt ashamed of my own reluctance to rise early when I reflected that Yvette had been obliged to get up even earlier in order to make the journey out from the town to Aubépine – and she was simply doing it out of kindness!

It was still dark when we started our journey down the hill of Aubépine, but dawn was breaking as we passed through the sleeping town. My own tiredness vanished as I watched a cloudless sky brighten in the east. The day was full of promise and as the morning lightened so too did our spirits. Along our route, the early sun caught the infinitesimal drops of dew on the hedgerows, so that the hawthorn – the *aubépine* – sparkled with a thousand jewels. As the temperature rose, we rolled down the windows and birdsong merged with the blue and gold of that perfect May morning. It was a '*Pippa Passes*' sort of day; God was in his heaven and all was, for the moment, right with my world.

Around noon, we pulled off the motorway and began to drive along a small country road, looking for a place to picnic. Before long, we found the perfect spot: a shady patch of grass in a copse of trees at the entrance to a field. Glad to stretch our stiff limbs, we climbed from the car – Marie-Jeanne, who was a bad traveller and was obliged throughout the journey to exercise mind over matter, even gladder than the rest of us – and spread a rug on the ground for our meal. As usual, Claudine, apparently fearing that we would die of starvation on the journey, had provided us with a feast: cold chicken, lettuce fresh from the garden, tomatoes, a little white wine for the non-drivers, wonderfully runny cheese from the nearby Trappist monastery. A sense of contentment and companionability possessed me as I sat there in the sun beside Angèle, and looked affectionately across at Marie-Jeanne. The three of us had come through a lot together; we were like battle-scarred old soldiers on leave from the trenches.

All too soon, it was time to move on. There was still quite a distance to go and we needed to hurry if we were to visit Alençon and get to Lisieux by mid-afternoon, which was our plan. Without further delay we pressed on, reaching Alençon about 1.30.

The family home of St Thérèse was an interesting place, but somehow it did not affect me in the way her home in Lisieux – *Les Buissonets* – had done on the couple of occasions on which I had visited it. Her spirit seemed to linger in *Les Buissonets*, perhaps because she had known such an intensity of experience there. She had been only three years old when she had left Alençon and I could not feel that she had left much of an impression upon her birthplace. While we were wandering around the house, which is a sort of museum, a couple of American tourists came in. Approaching us, they asked if we spoke English. I was the only one who did. They wanted to know if we were 'real' Carmelites and, delighted to learn that we were, they took our photos. So on somebody's slide show somewhere in the United States, I am for ever a real Carmelite in the family home of St Thérèse in France. It is not true that the camera never lies!

It was about 4 o'clock when we finally rolled into the grounds of *l'Hermitage* at Lisieux and the first person I saw was my old friend Clothilde, the postulant from Paris, now arrayed, like myself, in the habit of a novice. I leaped out of the car to embrace her happily. I was looking forward to exchanging experiences with her. But there would be plenty of time for that over the next few days, as Marie-Jeanne reminded me. Now it was time to say goodbye to Yvette and get installed in our new quarters. One of the strangest aspects of this visit for me – as indeed it must have been for the others – was the fact that we were no longer living in enclosure, but were out in public. For the first time, I became aware that the people we met saw me as a nun, and I found it an odd and slightly disconcerting experience.

We went to bed early that night, tired from our pre-dawn start and from the long journey. I slept like a baby.

The next few days were full of new and deeply emotional experiences. Every morning the assembled novices – fifty of us – attended mass, celebrated by a Carmelite priest, Père Olivier Rousseau, who was, together with three Carmelite nuns, one of the organisers of the conference. For Angèle and me it was quite an experience to be among so many other novices, accustomed as we were to the small community of Aubépine. After mass, the morning was taken up with lectures and workshops, and after lunch our time was usually free until about 5 o'clock. This allowed us to visit the various places connected with St Thérèse, including the Basilica, the Carmel and *Les Buissonets*.

The lectures were excellent and, like the community retreat at Aubépine the previous December, seemed almost to have been planned with me in mind. Père Rousseau explained how Thérèse's doctrine of confidence in God sprang precisely from her realisation that there was an immense gulf between what she was and what she wanted to be. She accepted reality, said Père Rousseau; she knew that alone, she could never achieve what she aimed for. But it was precisely in her own incapacity that she found the reason for total confidence in God and complete abandonment of herself to him, who, she believed, would never have given her desires that he did not intend to fulfil.

This was infinitely encouraging to me, who by now seemed rooted in that very place of utter inability to improve. But it was in the talk given to us by Soeur Marie-Thérèse of the Carmel of Frileuse that I found something that lit a light, which, even in the very dark days that were yet to come, was never totally extinguished.

According to Soeur Marie-Thérèse, the mercy of God never comes to us without asking our consent. God's mercy places itself at our disposal; it begs for our love, it seeks a weak place, some crack or fissure, in us through which to enter. Quoting from a book called *Le Combat de Jacob* by M.-D. Molinié (Les Editions du Cerf, 1993), Soeur Marie-Thérèse said that through this fissure 'the Holy Spirit breathes a sigh that we do not understand. This may give rise in us to vague feelings of dissatisfaction, of aridity, or may even result in a new outbreak of certain faults, betraying thus the disarray of a soul in which the great battle has commenced' (my own translation). She went on to explain that this fissure is different for everyone and is often the very thing that we refuse to acknowledge exists in us – the thing we are most in denial about. God's mercy comes to meet us in the very place where we believe we are unable to love, unable to go to God. We think that if that particular fault or weakness were removed, everything would be much better. We cannot bring ourselves to believe that it is precisely that weakness which will lead us to God.

As I listened, I began to have a faint inkling of what might have been happening on the Day of the Old Beds and why I had been so helpless in spite of all my prayers. I realised that Soeur Marie-Thérèse had said something of great moment, the full implications of which had not yet dawned on me. I decided I would ask Marie-Jeanne to get *Le Combat de Jacob* for me when we got back to Aubépine, if we didn't already have it in the library. Some light had shone inside me, and I wanted to explore the interior terrain while it was shining brightly.

Throughout the conference, groups of novices were being organised to visit the Lisieux Carmel, so as to have an opportunity to see the places where St Thérèse had lived, worked, prayed and died. This was an opportunity that I had never had during my earlier visits to Lisieux, as lay people were not permitted to enter the enclosure of the Carmel. So it was with huge anticipation that I joined ten others on the afternoon of the third or fourth day of the conference and walked the short distance down the main road to the Carmel.

The redbrick building was different in every possible way from the one I had left behind in Aubépine. The Lisieux Carmel had been built in the nineteenth century, while the Carmel of Aubépine was only thirty years old. The Lisieux Carmel was situated on a busy road in the centre of a bustling town, whereas in Aubépine, the monastery was hidden in the woods at the top of a hill deep in the countryside, with its nearest neighbour more than a kilometre away. The Lisieux Carmel was a solid heavy building without architectural merit, sitting incongruously almost on the footpath, while that of Aubépine was beautiful in its simplicity and at one with the nature that surrounded it.

At the door, we were met by the prioress; she was to be our guide during the short tour. She led us through the enclosure door that Thérèse had passed through on the day of her entrance. Moved, I stood for a moment and imagined the scene I had so often read about, as the young girl – a child, really – tore herself away from the father she loved so much and passed through that door, her heart beating so wildly that she thought, as she herself recounts, that she was going to die. I remembered how I had felt myself when, on my eighteenth birthday, I had left my own parents outside the enclosure door of a Carmel that, in those early post-Vatican II days, had changed very little from the Carmels of Thérèse's time. My heart too had pounded so hard that I felt everyone could hear it. I remembered how, while I waited with my parents in the monastery parlour beforehand, my father had walked back and forth, back and forth, across the small room, absent-mindedly putting a coin in the poor box each time he passed it, until even the frozen face of my mother had relaxed for a moment and we had all laughed, easing the appalling tension.

The prioress brought us through the monastery and the small garden, pointing out places of interest as we passed. In the refectory, we were shown where Thérèse used to sit. There was nothing special about it; no plaque marked the spot. Some present-day member of the community now sat there. We were invited to sit there for a moment if we wished. Always one for touching stones and relics and putting my hand into ancient cracks in rocks and trees, I took up the offer. I did the same in the choir, as the nuns' part of the chapel is called, sitting in Thérèse's stall where she had prayed every day during the nine years she had spent in the monastery. Then we went to her cell, preserved as it was in her time, where, this time to the laughter of all present, I was specially invited to sit on the low stool where she had sat writing *The Story of a Soul*.

Finally, we made our way to the infirmary and to the room where she had died. It too is maintained today exactly as it was at the time of her death and is not in use for practical purposes. I stood inside the door of that rather gloomy room with its restricted view over part of the garden and imagined the young woman who lay there dying at the age of twenty-four. How must she have felt? During her last illness, she had undergone a severe trial of faith. She whose faith had been so strong that it had almost approached vision, had for the two years prior to her death lost all ability on any sensible level to imagine an afterlife, a loving God. Yet she never wavered in her prayer or her belief that, in spite of how she felt, there was indeed a God who was her loving Father, who awaited her in another life where all would be joy. How did she manage to cling to this during the pain, sickness, weakness and depression of the last stages of tuberculosis in those days in which there was no cure for that awful disease? I suddenly found that I was in tears, so strong was the sense of her presence and so vivid the impression of her personality at that time. Looking around somewhat shame-facedly as I blew my nose, I was relieved to see that I was not the only affected person in the company.

For the rest of that day, I was haunted by the thought of Thérèse, whose belief in God was so strong that it stood firm in the face of physical and psychological weakness. Thinking of her, I was reminded of another French Carmelite whom I had always loved, and whose name I had borne during my first essay at the Carmelite life: Elisabeth of the Trinity, a nun of the Carmel of Dijon. Elisabeth Catez was born in 1880, making her seven years younger than Thérèse. Up to the time of her entrance into Carmel, her life on the surface was very different to that led by the young Thérèse before her entrance. Elisabeth was the eldest of two children, her sister Marguerite being just two years younger. Their father died when Elisabeth was still a small child and her mother set about doing all she could on the limited pension of an army officer's widow to give the two girls all the advantages possible. Her wide circle of friends enabled her to bring them travelling every summer, staying with friends and relations throughout France and in Switzerland. Elisabeth greatly enjoyed these journeys. Very different in personality from Thérèse, she was sociable, outgoing and charming and made friends easily. She played tennis, went dancing, and was a talented pianist; at one stage of her life even being destined for a professional career in music. But she too was haunted by the Infinite and much to her mother's displeasure entered the Carmel of Dijon at the age of twenty-one.

A profound mystic, Elisabeth sank into the contemplative life as into her element. Riveted by the mystery of a trinitarian God, her short life was devoted to penetrating ever more deeply the depths of that mystery. Five years after her entrance she died of

Addison's disease, for which at that time a cure had not yet been found. She was beatified in the 1980s.

The Carmel where she lived in Dijon no longer exists. The community has moved a short distance away to a more modern building, but, as with Thérèse and Lisieux, the spirit of Elisabeth lives on in her native town. Her remains lie in her parish church of St Michel in Dijon and the nuns, when moving to their new home, had the very American idea of dismantling her cell and reassembling it in the new premises, where it has become a place of pilgrimage. Blessed Elisabeth of the Trinity does not have the popular attraction of St Thérèse, but she has always drawn those of a contemplative disposition who find a wonderful depth in her writings and great encouragement in her life. I too had visited the Carmel of Dijon and had been drawn under Elisabeth's spell.

In Lisieux, Angèle and I had a greater opportunity to spend time together than we normally had, as there was no rule of silence during the conference. A certain reserve that had always been evident in her dealings with me in the novitiate had disappeared and I saw a side of her that was unsuspected until now, lively and fun-loving. There was a sense of esprit de corps also; we were the Aubépine novices. The others were The Rest.

One of the things I had been most anxious to do during the *sessions* was to talk to other novices of my own age, to see whether they had problems like mine and, if so, how they coped with them. Clothilde from Paris was the person I talked to most. She was one of the two postulants who had come to spend a week in Aubépine during my first *stage* there and who had taken part with us in the pilgrimage to the Marian shrine. During that visit, I had got to know her very well and to like her very much. She was a few years older than me, but her background was very different as she had previously been married. Before I returned to Luxembourg at the end of my second *stage* I had visited her in her own Carmel, and stayed overnight in a cell with a view of the Eiffel Tower. Now I was meeting her again for the first time in over a year, and I was very anxious to find out how things had gone for her in the meantime.

It was something of a blow to discover that she seemed to have had a cloudless passage though her postulancy and novitiate up to that point. Somehow, I had come to believe that all my difficulties stemmed from the fact that I was older than the average novice and, because of that, found it hard to submit to the restrictions of life in the novitiate. But here was Clothilde, a woman who had reared a family, telling me that she had not experienced any serious problems at all since her entrance. Shaken, I realised that I needed to look more closely at the nature of my own difficulties.

However, the denial mechanism which had been somewhat weakened by my conversation with Clothilde kicked back into action again as a result of meeting Anna, another woman of my own age, who was at that time a postulant. Anna was from Eastern Europe, and so, like me, was a foreigner in France (another fact that I clung to as an explanation for my own difficulties). When we met in Lisieux, she was seriously doubting her ability to continue. As I had never quite reached that point, I was greatly and somewhat shamefully cheered to find someone worse than myself and I formulated the theory, which I expounded to Anna at some length, that the combination of age and language difficulties was the principal cause of our problems. According to my reasoning, Clothilde, who was French, was the proof that either of these factors alone was not sufficient to be a serious disturbance.

Grateful for any plank to cling to in the wreckage that was her postulancy, my new friend espoused this theory with enthusiasm. She would stick it out for a little longer, she said, expressing the view that our meeting was providential, as it gave her enough hope to believe that her difficulties were surmountable. (She may well have been correct in this opinion, because she did struggle on, and was in the end able to overcome all difficulties. She has since made her profession of vows in the community to which she belonged and recently became mistress of novices there.) So it was that once again I convinced myself that all would be well and that I was where I was meant to be for the rest of my life.

On the afternoon of our last day Angèle and I had a pleasant surprise. The Lisieux Carmel had at that time one novice; we had become quite friendly with her and with one or two other novices. At the afternoon tea-break, the Lisieux novice asked the four or five of us if we would like to come to the community recreation in the Carmel that evening. Needless to say, we all accepted with alacrity and so it was that we managed a second visit inside the enclosure of St Thérèse's Carmel. It made a fitting and happy end to our stay.

PART FIVE

'God only knows, God makes his plan, the information's unavailable to the mortal man'

Paul Simon, *'Slip slidin' away'*

Chapter 27

Suddenly, as it seemed to me, it was the summer of 1997. I found it difficult to grasp the fact that I had spent almost a year and a half in Aubépine. In spite of all my difficulties, I felt as though I had known the nuns all my life. Often, looking at them, I wondered whether they, like me, ever found community life difficult. If they did, they concealed it better than I did. I felt that the time had come to do a little stocktaking in relation to my experiences so far, and the opportunity to do so came about in an unexpected way.

One morning, Marie-Jeanne told us that we were going to have a novitiate holiday. Each of us in turn would have three days to do with as we pleased. There would be no work and no classes in the novitiate. We would not have to come to the chapel for prayer unless we wanted to; instead, we could pray in the woods or in the garden. We could relax, go to bed early, take our meals out of doors, do whatever we felt would help us to un-wind – 'within limits, of course,' she added, looking at me rather pointedly. She explained that this was a practice she had introduced into the life of the novitiate because she found that the first year and a half was generally difficult, and a break from routine seemed to help. Angèle, whose enthusiasm for commu-nity life was always strong, was a bit dubious about the idea of a holiday away from the community, but I was wholeheartedly enthusiastic and looked forward to three days of blissful solitude.

However, Angèle cheered up when Marie-Jeanne suggested to her that she might like to go camping for her holiday. The novitiate possessed a tent, which we spent a hilarious evening erecting at the edge of the woods. Here Angèle spent her three days, picking her way carefully each evening through the dark garden after the night office, armed with a flashlight, and spending her morning prayer time in the woods. It brought her back to her scouting days and she loved it.

During Angèle's holiday, I was alone with Marie-Jeanne in the novitiate. I had always found novitiate classes difficult; the atmosphere reminded me of school, with the two of us sitting side by side before Marie-Jeanne, being lectured to. I resented being treated like a child, as I saw it, and, as always, my resentment affected the general dynamic. But with Angèle absent, it was different. The lectures turned into discussions between Marie-Jeanne and me and I began to enjoy them. We were at that time studying St Matthew's Gospel and, at about this time, we came to the Sermon on the Mount. I was greatly struck by the first beatitude: 'Blessed are you who are poor.' It seemed in a strange way to fit my inner life as it then was: a life that was despoiled, impoverished, without the luxury of the masks and false self-images I had worn for so long. According to Jesus, this was a blessed life and I felt that I was on the brink of some enormous discovery.

Angèle returned from her holiday and it was my turn. I declined with thanks Marie-Jeanne's half-serious offer of the tent, explaining that I had never camped out in my life and was not about to start in my declining years. However, as the essence of the holiday was a change from routine, I thought that what I would most like to do was take a book and a packed lunch off down the fields each afternoon (weather permitting) and simply relax. Marie-Jeanne agreed with this plan and as an added holiday activity suggested that I might like to do some recreational (as opposed to spiritual) reading. I liked this idea, but was puzzled as to where I might find reading of a non-spiritual kind, never having seen any in the library of the monastery. I had reckoned without Marie-Jeanne's ingenuity. From a cupboard in the novitiate that I had never explored she produced a full set of the *Tintin* books in the original French. (For those who don't know, Tintin is a cartoon reporter created by the Belgian cartoonist Hergé around the time of the Second World War. Together with his dog Milou and his friends, the irascible Captain Haddock and the two policemen Dupond and Dupont – collectively known as *'les Dupondt'* – Tintin had a series of remarkable adventures involving trips to exotic lands and even to the moon.) Reading the *Tintin* books is an excellent way to learn colloquial, if somewhat dated, French and of amassing a wonderful collection of the colourful though harmless invectives beloved of Captain Haddock. So it was that in the first year of my novitiate, I found myself sitting in the sun in a field in the country, eating apples and chocolate and reading a comic. As far as I could remember, the last time I had done anything like that I had been about twelve years of age.

The three days were sheer bliss. All anxiety, all stress, seemed to slide away from my shoulders and from my heart. On the morning of the third day, I knew that the time had come to look more closely at the reasons why.

My sense of well-being was clearly not entirely due to *Tintin*. Looking back, I realised that I had felt exactly the same during the retreat before my *prise d'habit* and, to a lesser extent, during the Lisieux *sessions*. It was how I had felt during my stay in hospital, and looking even further back, it was how I had habitually felt when living in Luxembourg. The conclusion was inescapable: I was not, as a rule, happy and relaxed when with the community. I tried to face this unpleasant fact and to interrogate myself about the reasons. It seemed to me that there were two possible reasons: the first was that I was quite simply a person who preferred my own company and found it stressful to live with others; the second was that I was selfish, and needed to make a greater effort.

I argued the thing this way: if the first reason was the correct one, then if, as I believed, God was calling me to the contemplative life, he would help me to overcome my natural inclination to solitariness and enable me to live in a community without undue stress. That this hadn't happened so far meant either that this was not the real reason for my problems or that the present difficulties were all part and parcel of the breaking-down of my false self-image. If, on the other hand, the second reason was the true one, then I just had to fight harder against my selfishness.

The discerning reader will by now have seen the defect in this reasoning: it was all based on the premise that I had to continue living in the monastery and this in turn was based on my belief that this was the only way in which I could live a contemplative life. I was not yet ready to consider any alternative. Indeed, I didn't believe that there was an alternative; it seemed to me that all that had happened since the moment of revelation on the balcony of my apartment had led towards Aubépine. I was meant to be there; I was absolutely sure of it.

Chapter 28

The novitiate holiday was the last period of happiness I was to know at Aubépine. When I returned to the novitiate, rested and full of good resolutions, I was met with the news that work on the enclosure fence was to recommence the following week. We were at that time at the start of a heat wave and, alarmed, I asked Marie-Jeanne if it was really envisaged that we would carry out heavy work in such heat. Apparently it was: Marie-Jeanne said we had to start erecting the fence now, otherwise the area we had cleared would become overgrown again and the holes that had been drilled with such difficulty would become choked up.

The work that was now due to begin would be much more difficult than that of simply clearing undergrowth; worse still, it now appeared that the help we had hoped to get from male friends of the community was unlikely to be forthcoming for the most part. The components of the fence had been delivered to the monastery some weeks before and were lying in the garden covered by a huge tarpaulin. We would have to transfer the heavy iron posts and six-foot high rigid mesh sections down to the area where holes had been drilled at the Prairie, insert the posts in the holes, fill the holes first with stones and then with cement, thus securing the posts. Then would come the delicate business of fitting and securing the heavy mesh sections to the posts: all of this would have to be carried out in heat of over thirty degrees Celsius. All my forebodings returned and I was filled with a generalised anxiety that flitted from one awful imaginary prospect to another. The sisters would get heatstroke.

Marie-Jeanne, whose health was never very good, would do too much and make herself seriously ill … Panic rose in me, and I began to feel that I couldn't bear it. How would I ever get through the summer?

The new phase of the work on the enclosure fence began on the following Monday. I had spent the weekend in a state of acute anxiety, hoping against hope that something would happen to prevent the work going ahead as planned – torrential rain, for example. It is difficult now to pinpoint exactly what my real worry was (if there was any real worry, other than the increasing stress of trying to live a way of life for which I was totally un-fitted), but, whatever the reality, my reaction was out of all proportion. On Monday morning, my hope for a downpour was dashed the moment I woke up. My cell was filled with brilliant sunlight, the thin brown curtains doing little to impede its passage through the window. I got up and, pulling back the curtain, looked out hopelessly. The sky was white with the heat of the coming day and the temperature was already high. As I gazed at the parched grass, a strange buzzing began in my ears. I was not going to be able to face the day. What was I to do? I sat on the edge of the bed and tried to be rational. What, after all, was going to happen? A group of us were going to carry some heavy metal posts and insert them in holes that had already been drilled. Others were going to fill the holes with cement. We would spend about three hours at this and then we would return to the monastery for the midday office and lunch. After lunch we would have an hour's spiritual reading in our cells, then we would head off to the fields again, where we would work for two more hours before returning for evening prayer. What was there to be afraid of in this programme? Nothing, it seemed, yet I was terrified. The thing had got completely out of hand, and I didn't understand why.

Shakily I made my way downstairs to the chapel for prayer,

but there was to be no peace that morning. Thoughts tumbled chaotically around in my head. At six, it was already hot and stuffy in the chapel; what would it be like in the full glare of the day down in the open fields?

At breakfast, I couldn't eat. I saw Marie-Jeanne glancing at me once or twice and I wondered if I looked as strange as I felt. I went back upstairs to my cell to change into jeans and a tee shirt, I felt remote, disembodied, yet at the same time, panicky. I could not seem to get enough air into my lungs. Taking deep breaths, I went down to join the others who were assembled at the back door waiting for Thérèse to bring the tractor and trailer around. They were all laughing and chatting and I tried desperately to feel a part of it. Marie-Paule was staying behind to mix the cement in the brand new cement-mixer we had purchased, and which we had christened Hercules (a companion for Samson the tractor).

Thérèse and Samson arrived, followed by Marie-Jeanne with the car. Getting out to help with loading the trailer, she came over to me and asked if I was all right.

'Perfectly!' I assured her, trying to sound eager and ready for work. She looked at me a little anxiously, but didn't pursue the matter. We loaded up the trailer with heavy metal posts and some of the mesh fencing. I wished desperately that I could ease the fluttering feeling around my heart. I continued my deep breathing until I noticed Thérèse looking at me. The day was hot and breathless, not a leaf moved on any tree. Perhaps that was why I felt unable to breathe properly, I told myself encouragingly. At least one good thing had happened: the sun had temporarily disappeared behind a heavy grey haze.

When the trailer was full, Angèle climbed in to make sure that nothing fell off en route and she and Thérèse set off down the drive. I watched them go, feeling that I was no part of any of it. What had gone so wrong? *How* had it gone so wrong?

Oh, please help me, please help me. I am alone and afraid. I seem to have lost my way on this journey. Where are You? Why have You left me like this? Don't You care that I'm wandering in a desert, unable to find the path I was on before? I don't know when I strayed from that path; I didn't even know I had left it until I looked around one day and saw nothing but the wilderness. But I know You are there some- where. I know that You are with me, even if I walk in the Valley of Darkness. But couldn't You give me just a little sign of Your presence? Then everything would be so much easier to bear.

When the tractor had left, Véronique got into the car beside Marie-Jeanne, I climbed into the back and we drove off. By the time we reached the Prairie, the others had begun to unload the trailer. Anxious to face the worst (that mysterious, shadowy worst) as soon as possible, I rushed to help them and began heaving the heavy metal posts onto the ground. Before long I was bathed in perspiration, but I didn't care. I was facing the fear and everything would be all right. I thought of the medieval English mystic, Julian of Norwich.

'All will be well,' she thought she had heard God say to her, 'and all will be well, and all manner of things will be well.' I repeated it to myself like a mantra.

When all the posts and rigid sections of fence were on the ground, the really tricky part began. We had to carry them down the steep narrow track to the area we had cleared at the bottom of the hill. By the time we had made the difficult journey three or four times, three of us struggling down Indian file with one long metal post balanced across three sets of shoulders, we were already tired. My shoulder was aching from the weight of the post and my calves were aching from the descent. Here was a new fear – perhaps I would snap another tendon? In spite of all my anxiety, I had to laugh at myself. This was becoming too ridiculous!

Bringing the material down the hill was proving so difficult that Véronique decided we would erect what we had brought down so far and then take a rest before bringing down any more. But the new task proved to be no less strenuous. Each post had to be set in the prepared hole and hammered into place. Then two people had to hold it steady, while two more filled up the hole with stones before finally pouring in the cement. Up to that point, although the day was hot and humid, it was also overcast, so we had been spared the direct glare of the sun. But now the clouds parted and the fierce August sun shone down upon us with unrelenting fury. My dizziness increased. I felt as though I were floating away. The voices of the others and the ringing sound of the hammer hitting iron seemed to come from a great distance. Terror seized me; some unknown horror seemed to be lurking. My heart began to palpitate and I sat down suddenly. I didn't know what was happening to me. I didn't recognise the symptoms of a panic attack; I'd never had one before.

Marie-Jeanne came over.

'I'm fine,' I said, before she could speak, 'I'm fine.' My breath was coming in little gasps.

'You're not fine,' Marie-Jeanne said. 'Come and sit under the trees for a while.'

I protested. At all costs I did not want to give in. In some vague, muzzy way, I felt that it would be fatal to do so. But Marie-Jeanne insisted.

'It's time we all took a break anyway,' she said, and clapping her hands she summoned the others. Everyone collapsed onto the grass under the trees, laughing and groaning. The picnic basket was opened; cold drinks and biscuits were unpacked. I sat with my back propped against a tree, not wanting to speak, cautiously flexing my interior muscles and testing my psyche for broken bones. I seemed to be in one piece. The dizziness was fading, but I felt as if I were recovering from an illness.

'All will be well, and all will be well, and all manner of things will be well,' I repeated to myself.

Marie-Jeanne and Véronique were whispering to one another.

I knew they were going to suggest that I go back to the house. I didn't want to go. Here was another thing I couldn't understand. I didn't want this work to go ahead at all, but if it had to, then I wanted to be part of it. Somewhere in this confused thinking was the childish notion that if I could survive it, everyone else would too; but if I wasn't there, goodness knows what awful things might happen. And somewhere in it too was the old fear of being left out.

Véronique and Marie-Jeanne had finished their conversation. Véronique came and sat down beside me.

'Would you like to go back to the house?' she asked kindly.

'No thanks, really, I'm fine,' I said, as firmly as I could, although to my surprise my voice didn't have much strength in it. I still seemed to be short of breath.

Véronique looked at me for a moment.

'Well, all right,' she said quietly. 'But I don't want you to do any more of that heavy work. There's a patch of undergrowth over there that needs clearing. It would be a help if you could do that.'

The patch of undergrowth in question was in the shade. Grateful that Véronique had not insisted I go back, I went across and began to clear the light brush. I found I had to work slowly; my limbs were strangely weak.

When we went back to the monastery for lunch, Marie-Jeanne said she wanted to see me in the novitiate. Fearing the worst, I went.

'I really don't want you to do any more work on the fence,' said Marie-Jeanne. 'I think it's too much for you.'

I protested vehemently, but she was adamant.

'Look, I'll take a rest this afternoon, and then I'll be fine tomorrow. Please!' I begged.

'Well', Marie-Jeanne wavered a bit. 'Take a rest, and we'll see. But I really feel that you shouldn't continue.'

Relieved, I left her. All the same, I was glad enough after lunch to go to my cell and lie on my bed while the others set off back down the fields – as long, of course, as I could rejoin them the following day. I felt that it was absolutely imperative that I get back into some sort of ordinary routine, so that I could begin to feel part of the community again. For otherwise, I knew, everything would be lost.

Chapter 29

Tuesday was another hot and humid day. I hadn't slept very much the previous night. At breakfast, I looked expectantly at Marie-Jeanne. She shook her head. She was sticking firmly to yesterday's position: I was not to join in the work today. I felt my chest tighten and the old anger and helplessness rise up inside me like a physical thing. Suddenly, I couldn't finish my coffee and roll. I had to talk to Marie-Jeanne; I had to persuade her to let me go with the others. I quickly washed my plate and bowl and made a sign to her that I wanted to speak to her outside. Frowning, she put down her half-eaten roll and followed me. Outside, I tried to calm down and marshal my thoughts.

'Please let me go with the others today, Marie-Jeanne,' I began. 'I feel fine.'

'No,' she replied firmly. 'I told you, I think it's too much for you.'

I began to argue with her hopelessly. Her face closed up in the old familiar way and I knew it was useless. The inner battle began. Let it go, I told myself. Here's where you can hand over your will to God. Perhaps he has picked this moment to be the breakthrough. But try as I might, *pray* as I might, the only reality in the world just then was my despair and anger at being left out. It was the Day of the Old Beds all over again. Marie-Jeanne recognised this and even tried to joke about it.

'Let go of the bed, Noreen!' she urged, smiling at me. But I was too far gone to respond. Her smile faded as it met my stony glare. She turned to go. 'I'm not going to discuss this any further,' she said firmly as she left.

I went to my cell and tried to focus. I was aware that things

144

were getting hopelessly out of hand. I was in total turmoil, and I knew that it was unjustified. I needed to regain a sense of proportion. I sat on the stool in front of the window and gazed unseeingly upon the woods beyond the garden. How had I reached this pitch? I wondered. Where now was all the idealism and enthusiasm of my early visits to Aubépine? The place where I was to find the Beloved had revealed itself to be a place of demons. I closed my eyes, and tried to find the One I loved.

> Whither hast thou hidden thyself, and hast left me, O Beloved, to my sighing?

The words which had first touched me in Luxembourg came to my mind, but where was all the joy and longing that they had then aroused in me? Now they seemed to echo in an empty wasteland and I sat bleakly before the ruin of my dreams. I could not see any way back to that place of happiness.

> Quench thou my griefs, since none suffices to remove them,
> and let mine eyes behold thee, since thou art their light
> and for thee alone I wish to have them.

I closed my eyes and tried to escape into that silent inner citadel. For a moment, I thought I was going to succeed. A stillness began to creep over my tumultuous thoughts, but even as, almost unconsciously, I relaxed my guard, the loud querulous voices began again. 'They've gone off and left you out yet again. It's not fair! There is no reason why you should have to put up with that sort of treatment. You are within your rights in telling them how you feel! Who are they to say what you are able for or what you are not able for? Surely you're the only one who can say that? Anyway, they're only using that as an excuse, to make it look as if they care about you, while what they're really trying to do is isolate you more and more, so that in the end, you will leave. That's what they really want; they've never really accepted you!'

I don't know how long I sat there listening to those horrible voices, but the longer I sat, the more I agreed with them. They were right! This was intolerable, and I did not have to tolerate it! Once and for all I would make Marie-Jeanne understand this when she returned from the field that evening.

I don't remember much about the rest of that day; it passed in a blur. The team must have returned for the midday office and meal as usual, but I have no recollection of it. Neither do I remember how I occupied myself, or whether I carried out my usual daily tasks. External events were only the background to the epic inner battle that continued throughout the day as I tried to fight against the dreadful voices. Now and again, reason (and, I hope, God) seemed for a moment to regain the upper hand and it was as though I emerged for a moment from a dark place underground into the sweet-smelling, sunlit air. In those brief moments, I recognised the irrationality of my earlier thoughts and knew once again why I was in the monastery and Who it was that I had come to seek. And then the darkness came down again and nothing mattered except my battered and bruised self.

Finally, the evening of that long day came. The heat and humidity had intensified, banks of purple clouds had appeared on the horizon and rumbles of thunder could be heard in the distance. I rang the bell for prayer at 5 o'clock and looked around the stifling choir. Apart from Claudine, the infirmarian, only the aged and infirm were present. And me, of course, I thought bitterly, as I went to kneel in my usual place. But as Claudine began the invocation of the Holy Spirit which always started our prayer, the choir door opened and Marie-Jeanne came in and went to her place. My heart drummed so loudly in my ears that I was almost deafened. I was sure everyone could hear it. It was so loud that I could no longer think. All I knew was that I could not bear to kneel there for another moment without telling Marie-Jeanne how I felt. I got up and went across to where she was sitting. She looked up, surprised.

'Marie-Jeanne, I need to talk to you,' I said urgently. 'Can you come out for a moment?'

This was unprecedented, but something in my face must have made her realise that she had better do as I asked. She got up and went out. I followed her, and she led me into the nearby *avant-choeur*, the small room where we kept our breviaries and white cloaks.

'Well,' she asked, 'what is it?'

I realised I didn't know where to begin; indeed, I was finding it difficult to speak at all. My feelings had risen up and were filling my throat and choking me. But I tried anyway.

'It's about today,' I began, as I felt tears start to my eyes. Marie-Jeanne's own eyes flashed dangerously behind her glasses.

'Noreen,' she said quietly, 'please don't start that again.'

'But I just don't understand,' I insisted. 'All I'm looking for is an explanation. I just want to know why you think I'm not able for the work on the fence when everyone else is. It can't be my age. You consider that you're able yourself, for example, but you're older than I am.'

'I don't have to explain anything to you,' said Marie-Jeanne coldly. 'You really are sailing very close to the wind. I advise you to stop now and go back into the choir.'

It was then that I lost all reason. Words suddenly flowed from me, with a fluency I hadn't known I possessed in French. All the accumulated resentment of months came out and was directed at poor Marie-Jeanne, who stood there, white-faced. Finally I ran out of words, and came gasping to a stop.

'Have you finished?' she enquired, her tone icy. I didn't reply. She said a few words which I no longer recall and then, in answer to some question of mine, gave a response which in my hyper-sensitive state I felt to be too facile. Extraordinarily, this answer of Marie-Jeanne's which was to be decisive for my future in Aubépine has passed so completely from my mind that I have not the slightest idea what it was, or indeed what the question was that had provoked it. But I remember well that, waving my hand airily, I said with a bitter smile,

'Oh, tu dirais n'importe quoi!'

This phrase, which can be translated as 'You'd say any old thing', has a force in French which is totally lacking in English. It is dismissive to the point of contempt and indicates that the opinions of your interlocutor are not worth consideration. The moment the words had left my mouth I wanted to withdraw them. I seemed to suddenly come to my senses with a sense of terrible shock. But it was too late. Marie-Jeanne had had more than enough and was walking out of the *avant-choeur*. In desperation I ran after her and caught her arm, babbling apologies.

'Let me go,' she said, her tone dangerous. I wouldn't. I felt that if I let her walk away now, it would be the end. Clinging to her arm, in tears and almost hysterical, I begged her to listen to me, protesting that I hadn't meant it, that I was so sorry.

'Let … me … go,' she said very deliberately, turning to face me, and I saw nothing but distaste and revulsion in her face. It was clear that she could not bear to remain near me for another second. Defeatedly, I released her and she walked out.

Now I had to face what I had done. I had treated the novice mistress with contempt. I had behaved unpardonably towards her and then practically held her prisoner against her will. I had reached a very low moment and I had no idea what to do next. There seemed to be only one refuge left. I went back into the choir and tried to pray.

Chapter 30

In one way, the whole episode had been cathartic. All my feelings of resentment had gone. I felt nothing now but sorrow for the hurt I had caused Marie-Jeanne and fear of the consequences. I was immensely tired; and feeling that I had broken so many rules now that one more wouldn't make any difference, I did not go into supper or recreation with the community, but instead went to my cell and went to bed. In spite of my exhaustion, I slept very little.

The next morning, I rose with the feeling that I absolutely must put everything right as soon as possible. When breakfast was over, I tried to catch Marie-Jeanne, but she left quickly and, before I could catch up with her, I saw her disappearing into Véronique's office. I went as usual to my cell for the period of spiritual reading which we always had at this time.

I was trying without much success to concentrate on my book when there was a knock at the door. It was Marie-Jeanne. I was delighted to see her and told her so. Rapidly, I explained how much I wanted to make amends for the previous day. I had been awake most of the night, I told her, and had thought a lot about everything and realised I had got everything out of perspective. I had allowed hurts and resentments to take over, but now I was anxious to start again.

Marie-Jeanne listened without interrupting. When I had finished, she looked at me, her eyes tired.

'Well,' she said, 'I didn't sleep very much last night either and I too have been thinking deeply about it all. But I have come to a different conclusion. I have concluded that this is not the place for you and that the time has come for you to recognise that and leave.'

Her voice seemed to be coming from a long distance away. For a moment I thought I was going to faint, so great was the shock. And then, gathering my forces, I began to plead, feeling as if I were pleading for my very life. Marie-Jeanne remained outwardly unmoved, though I know now how much the whole episode cost her. I asked her if she had said anything to Véronique. She had, of course, and Véronique wanted to see me at 11 o'clock. This news lit a flicker of hope inside me and I calmed down a little.

But the feeling of being in a nightmare was still with me when I knocked at the door of Véronique's office at the appointed time. When I went in, I was taken aback to see that Marie-Jeanne was also present. I would have preferred to see Véronique alone, but, feeling that I was in no position to make demands, I said nothing about it. Nevertheless, I felt that the battle-lines were being drawn up against me.

Véronique was very kind. She opened the proceedings by explaining that Marie-Jeanne had told her all about the events of the previous day and that she agreed with her that the time had come for me to recognise that the enclosed life was not for me. Nobody was blaming me in any way, she stressed, and I must not feel that I had failed. It was quite simply that my temperament was unsuited to the enclosed life. They all recognised that I had made enormous efforts, but the very fact that I had to try so hard was an indication that something was not right. The efforts I was making were causing me undue strain, she said, and she would be failing in her duty to me if I allowed it to continue.

It was all eminently reasonable, but I didn't believe a word of it and I didn't want to listen to any of it. She was wrong, wrong, my heart kept insisting passionately. She didn't understand. Finally she ended, and I began to speak. I argued and pleaded as I had never pleaded in court when I was a barrister. I reminded her of all the events that had led me to Aubépine. I asked her if

God's will was to be discounted just because I had not lived up to requirements. I said much more that I have now forgotten, but it was all summed up in four words: give me another chance. And before I left the room, she had reluctantly agreed to give me a month to see how things went. Promising fervently that I would change, I left the room feeling like someone reprieved from execution.

The rest of that day passed in a daze and in exhausting fluctuations of feeling. At one moment I was sure that everything would be all right, at the next, I was convinced that at the end of my month's probation, Véronique would still think I should leave. But I was now absolutely certain of one thing: I did not want to go. During prayer that evening, I implored God to change the minds of Véronique and Marie-Jeanne. If somewhere in the back of my mind there was an uneasy little voice suggesting that my own will might not be identical with God's, I quickly stifled it. How could it possibly be God's will for me to leave? He had made it clear to me that he wanted me to live a contemplative life; how could I do that if I were not here?

But that night I slept soundly. When I woke, I was filled with the thought of how I had jeopardised my future and all that God had planned for me. And it was all through selfishness and resentment. Now, however, everything was going to be different. I was like someone saved from drowning; I had had a huge shock, and all the petty hurts and disappointments had fallen into perspective. At breakfast, I smiled across the refectory at Marie-Jeanne (how easy it was to smile now!) and received a faint smile in return. My heart lifted. Everything was going to be all right, I was sure of it. I felt more peaceful and grounded than I had felt for weeks.

Back in my cell after breakfast, I looked out of the window at the sunny August morning. The trees in the forest had the dried-up look of the end of summer and the grass in the novitiate garden was yellow from the long drought. Under the window, the rose bushes that the three of us had planted the previous year were in bloom. In the distance, I could see the team setting off to work on the fence, and I watched them make their way to the car, laughing and chatting. It no longer mattered to me in the least that I was not with them. Marvelling, I reflected upon the change that had been wrought in me by the simple possibility of having to leave this place I loved so much. I picked up the book that I was reading. It was *Le Combat de Jacob*. Marie-Jeanne had got it for me after our return from Lisieux, when I told her how much the quotation from it in one of the talks had impressed me. I had only begun to read it in the last few days. I had reached a place where the author speaks about a time in the spiritual life when, if God is to be free to come to us without impediment on our side, we must be weaned away from everything we cling to instead of him. This, the author said, can affect us like an earthquake, shaking us up in the things we hold most dear, and above all, in the things we think are indispensable for our journey to God. As I opened the book now, my eye fell on the following passage:

> The precious pearl itself seems to be reduced to crumbs. We have sold everything in order to buy this pearl, intuiting God through certain realities for which we have sacrificed everything. And little by little, these realities are collapsing. (My own translation)

Shaken, I closed the book again. Could this really be true? Could it really be the case that the life I envisaged here at Aubépine had to be taken from me so that God could come to me? A great void seemed to open at my feet. This God for whom I was searching was a dangerous Lover. I could find no firm foothold on the road that led to wherever it was that he was waiting. Indeed, it was not a road; I seemed now to be walking upon shifting sands. I was still sitting there, gazing with unseeing eyes at the garden beyond my window, when Marie-Jeanne and Véronique arrived together.

Chapter 31

For a while, I could not take it in. They had come to tell me that the matter was now decided. I must leave; the only question was when.

'But you promised me a month,' I said desperately to Véronique.

'I've changed my mind,' she replied. 'Marie-Jeanne has persuaded me.'

I looked at Marie-Jeanne, the betrayer. She met my accusing gaze unflinchingly.

'It really is for the best,' she said quietly. 'You'll realise that in time.'

'How could it possibly be for the best?' I demanded wildly. 'I've given up everything to come here. I've no home, no job ...'

'You'll get another job,' Véronique interjected, a little weakly. 'You're highly qualified.'

They didn't care. They were washing their hands of me. They had decided I should go and they had no further interest in what happened to me. As I realised that this time there was no arguing with them, the tears began. Once I had started to cry, I couldn't stop. I cried as if my heart was breaking, and indeed it felt as if it was. Marie-Jeanne and Véronique sat there helplessly as I wept, as all the anguish and pain of the past year and a half poured out of my eyes in an unstoppable flood.

All through that terrible day I sat there at the table by the window of my cell, weeping. I attended none of the community exercises. I was vaguely aware that Marie-Jeanne came in from time to time and tried to talk to me, but I couldn't stop the agonising crying. At lunchtime she appeared with a meal on a tray: invalid food. I left it there, untouched. Finally, in the evening, alarmed by the unceasing tears, she called Véronique.

Véronique sat down beside me, took a handkerchief and began to wipe away the tears that were falling so heavily. I don't remember what she said to me, but I began to calm down for the first time. I was exhausted, and she suggested that I go to bed. I did; and unbelievably, I slept.

For the next few days, I couldn't bear to attend any of the community meals or recreations. I knew Véronique had told the sisters that I was leaving and I couldn't imagine how I would ever be able to hold a normal conversation with any of them again.

I don't remember when exactly Véronique began to take a firm line with me, but at some stage she came to my cell, pulled up a chair and said, 'Now, it's time to begin making some practical arrangements. First of all, where do you want to go when you leave here?'

I looked at her. 'I don't know,' I said weakly. 'Not back to Ireland, anyway.' I was quite certain at that moment that I could not return straight home from Aubépine. It was four years since I had lived in Ireland, and Luxembourg seemed more familiar just then. Yes, I thought, I would like to go back to Luxembourg. Maybe there, in the place where it had all begun, I could find peace again. Indeed, the more I thought about it, the more it seemed to be the right thing. I had been able to pray there once; surely I would again.

'I think I'll go back to Luxembourg,' I said now to Véronique. 'Perhaps I might be able to get a job at the Court again; I could ring and find out whether there are any openings.'

Pleased that I was at last beginning to show some enthusiasm for life after Aubépine, Véronique was loud in her encouragement.

'That seems like a great idea,' she said. 'Ring this morning and see what the story is. But in the meantime, do you think it might be a good idea to spend a couple of weeks somewhere quiet immediately after you leave, just to get accustomed to being outside again?'

I considered this proposition for a moment. It seemed attractive.

'Have you somewhere in mind?' I asked.

She had. 'I was thinking of the Trappistine Abbey in Chambarand, in the French Alps,' she said. 'It's in wonderful countryside, and you could visit St-Antoine, which is nearby, and is a very interesting old town. I'll get out the map this evening, and we can have a look at where it is.'

For the first time, I felt a flicker of interest as my old travelling and holiday instincts awoke. I agreed to go to Chambarand. Véronique told me that she had already contacted the Abbey and that they could fit me in for a fortnight in their guesthouse starting on 8 September. Suddenly I was panic-stricken; 8 September was only ten days away.

'I can't go so soon!' I exclaimed. 'I have to have time to get used to the idea ...' My voice trailed off into appalled silence.

Véronique was calm but firm. She saw no reason why I should stay a moment longer than was necessary to make all practical arrangements. She pointed out how difficult it would be for me to interact with the community once the decision had been made, and I had to agree. Indeed, at the moment, I was finding it next to impossible and I said so. This led Véronique to broach another topic.

'You really must try to rejoin the community for what's left of your time here,' she urged. 'The sisters are very upset about it all and it makes it even more difficult for them when you stay in your room like this. They want to be able to talk to you, and I do honestly feel that you would be the better for it yourself. So please try to come to recreation this evening.'

I felt resentment and resistance surge up in me again. Oh yes, I thought bitterly. Worry about the community and how they feel! Don't bother about me! But I fought it. I knew really that Véronique was thinking just as much about me as she was about the community. And, if the truth be told, I was beginning to get a little tired of the four walls of my cell. So, although I was apprehensive and ill at ease, I agreed to come to the evening recreation.

On summer evenings, recreation at Aubépine always took place in the garden. We used to assemble in a grassy spot shaded by trees at the edge of the forest and the routine invariably followed the same pattern. At the end of supper, Angèle, Marie-Paule and I would leave before everyone else and hurry out to the garden to set out the white plastic garden chairs that were kept stacked under the trees. We used to race each other down to get them assembled in a semicircle before the first of the sisters arrived, and this evening was no exception. In the exhilarating dash down the hill from the back door, my angst was temporarily forgotten and, in a split second of revelation, I realised that I was enjoying this brief moment of togetherness more than usual because the strain of community life was so soon to be lifted entirely from my shoulders. This flash of awareness of liberation passed almost before I grasped it, but when it had gone, something hopeful remained, like a little gem enclosed in a velvet purse; I knew I could take it out and look at it more carefully when the dark times returned.

And Véronique was right. Recreation was a great help. The sisters were kind and tactful and nobody mentioned my departure. The usual mundane things were discussed and gradually the sense of nightmare of the past few days began to lift. It was a little like returning to work after a great bereavement; there was that reassuring sense that life goes on, which is the faint beginning of healing. I didn't contribute much to the general conversation. I was content to sit there in the warm evening air, listening to the twittering of the birds as they prepared to retire for the night. Crickets were chirping quietly in the grass, a few bats swooped among the trees, the sky was a deep violet in the east and a kind of peace began to return to my heart. For a short while, I let go and relaxed. Marie-Jeanne looked across at me a couple of times and smiled and I was able to smile back.

As we walked back across the lawn to the monastery at the end of recreation, an enormous tiredness possessed me. It was the sort of tiredness I remembered from childhood holidays at the seaside, when at the end of a long sunny day, one returned sleepy and content to the guesthouse, bare feet hot and sandy inside one's sandals, mouth sticky from chocolate and ice cream. Bedtime was bliss on such an evening, and so it was tonight. I slept in my hard Carmelite bed like a 5-year-old child.

The next morning, I began to feel a return of energy. I telephoned the deputy registrar of the Court in Luxembourg, who was an Irishman and an old friend. I told him my situation and asked him whether there were any job vacancies in the offing. He promised to look into the matter and to get back to me without delay. He was warm, friendly and supportive, and wanted to know whether there was anything he and his wife could do to help. There wasn't, of course, but the very fact of their concern warmed me. I remembered that I had friends, both in Luxembourg and in Ireland, who would, in spite of their disappointment that things had not worked out for me, be delighted to see me again. Feeling much more positive now, my next task was to arrange for somewhere to live when my two weeks in Chambarand were over.

This was difficult. I would have a certain amount of money, as Véronique was going to give me back the money I had brought with me to contribute to the community. I would be able to support myself with this for a short time, until I got a job. However, Luxembourg was an expensive place for an unemployed person to live and I had to face the fact that I might be unemployed for some time. Yet I needed to be near at hand so as to be able to go there for interviews, if they arose. Balancing the pros and cons, I decided that the best thing would be to find a place to live on the

French side of the Luxembourg border, where the cost of living was lower. Then Véronique had the bright idea of consulting the Carmelite nuns in Metz, to see whether they knew of any rooms in the town that I could rent cheaply for a couple of months.

The Metz Carmelites turned up trumps. They had a friend who had just decided to let the ground floor of her house and she was happy to have me as her first tenant until such time as I got a job in Luxembourg. So it was arranged that after my two weeks in Chambarand I would move to her house in Chemin des Oiseaux in Metz. I liked the sound if it – 'Birds' Way'. Now that I had an address, the future didn't look quite so alarming. I still had no job, it was true, but I had a little money and I had a flat at Chemin des Oiseaux, Metz. I began to feel like a real person again.

Chapter 32

The days passed rapidly. I had written to my sister Eileen in Ireland to explain matters, asking her to tell Clare and Liam. But unknown to me until it was too late to do anything about it, Véronique had done the same thing, and unfortunately her letter reached Eileen before mine did, causing her some upset. However, I spoke to all three on the phone and reassured them that I was all right.

On Friday, three days before I was due to leave, a number of things happened. First, my friend the deputy registrar of the Court rang to tell me that there were no immediate vacancies there, but that if I could stay around for a while something might turn up. I told him that I would be living temporarily in Metz, and so would be easily able to go to Luxembourg if required. He took my new address and phone number and promised to get in touch if anything turned up. Although his news disappointed me, I was cheered by his warmth and friendliness and by the sensation of being back in some sort of familiar loop.

The next thing that happened was that Marie-Jeanne asked me if I would like to go with her into town the following day to get my hair cut and coloured. The wave of relief that poured over me at this proposal shamed me not a little. Had my year and a half of prayer and contemplation wrought so little change in me that the prospect of getting my hair coloured was sufficient to lift my spirits to such heights? So it was, however, and only then did I realise how daunting had been the prospect of appearing in public with all my grey roots showing. Indeed, vanity dies hard!

The third event of that day was almost comical in its

incongruity. I was in my cell after lunch, attempting to sort out my belongings – an activity which had induced another bout of tears – when Véronique knocked at the door to say that two Irish Carmelite priests had arrived and were asking for me. She had spoken to them briefly, but had not told them that I was on the verge of departure. Taken aback, because I hadn't been expecting any visitors, and indeed, knew no Irish Carmelite friars, I went down to the parlour. There I met two priests from Clarendon Street in Dublin who were on their way to Rome. One of them, a large, jovial man in his mid-fifties, explained that they had heard there was a Dublin woman in Aubépine and they had said to themselves that they absolutely must stop off there and say hello to her.

'Sure we were thinking you must feel a bit homesick from time to time, here among all these Frenchwomen!' he said.

I mentally reviewed the various comments I could make in response to this, but decided that there was no point in beating about the bush.

'Actually,' I said, shaking hands with them, 'you've come only just in time. If you'd been a few days later, I wouldn't have been here. I'm leaving on Monday.'

There was a second's silence while they glanced at one another, and then, disconcertingly, they burst into loud guffaws of laughter. No doubt their reaction was one of embarrassment more than anything else – I mean, what are the social niceties in such a situation? It's a little like the joke about the man who meets an old friend he hasn't seen for years, and asks him how his wife is.

'She's in heaven,' says the friend gravely.

'Oh, that's terrible!' says the first man, and then thinks that 'terrible' is hardly an appropriate adjective to describe the wife's celestial home.

'I mean,' he adds hastily, 'that's wonderful!'

I expect the two Irish priests felt a little bit like that man.

Actually, their reaction did me a power of good, so different was it from all the intensity of the past few days. Their laughter over, they didn't dwell on the matter, but expressed regret that I wasn't free to depart there and then, as they would, they said, have taken me with them to Rome, where I could have had 'a bit of a holiday', as they put it. Then they went on to fill me in on the news from Ireland and to tell me about their own trip. Finally they asked me to make a call to a hotel they were to stay in, changing the time of their booking. They were afraid to do it themselves in case whoever came to the phone didn't speak English. It was with regret that I saw them off an hour or so later. I had greatly enjoyed their visit.

During those dark days, prayer, for the first time, no longer provided a refuge and respite. I was convinced that what was happening was a huge mistake, all brought about because of my arrogance and selfishness in trying to assert my own will. In fact, this was the principal cause of the pain I was suffering; indeed, if I could have brought myself to believe that what was happening was part of God's plan for my life, I would have felt only relief at the prospect of liberation from the restraints of enclosed community life. But because I couldn't believe that, I didn't know how to present myself before God other than in an attitude of deep contrition. I had learned enough during the year and a half in the novitiate to believe that God, as a loving Father, forgives us instantly, whatever our faults, once we ask for his forgiveness. How was it then that I couldn't feel myself to be forgiven? I have often puzzled over my attitude to God during this period, and I can only think that he allowed my mind to be darkened in this way so that I could make the absolute act of trust which ultimately I did make: which was that he could, and *would*, draw good from what had happened, even if it was my own fault. But I would already have left Aubépine before I reached that point and it would be months before I recognised that my leaving had all been part of God's plan for me. St John of the Cross describes a similar experience in *Dark Night of the Soul*, when he says:

> For indeed, when this purgative contemplation is most severe, the soul feels very keenly the shadow of death and the lamentations of death and the pains of hell, which consist in its feeling itself to be without God, and chastised and cast out, and unworthy of him, and it feels that he is wroth with it. All this is felt by the soul in this condition – yea, and more, for it believes that it is so with it for ever. (Book II, Ch. VI)

A time would come when I would realise that everything had been leading me to this point and to the ultimate act of surrender that would be drawn from me. But that's a story for another day.

Chapter 33

On Saturday, I set off with Marie-Jeanne to the shopping centre where she was going to do the community's weekly shop and where I was to get my hair done. For the occasion, I got back into the civilian clothes I had worn as a postulant. On the way to the shopping centre, we stopped off at a small dry-cleaners, where I left in my old trench coat to be cleaned; I hadn't worn it since my entrance a year and a half earlier. Marie-Jeanne waited for me in the car. As I passed the coat over the counter to the assistant, I was struck by the familiarity of the gesture. I had done this so often in my life; it was one of the normal things one did, one of the countless tiny things that make up an adult life where one is responsible for oneself. I hadn't done it since I had entered Aubépine.

We separated when we reached the shopping centre. Marie-Jeanne went off to the supermarket and I went to make a few purchases before the time for my hairdressing appointment. The previous day I had gone with Thérèse to the bank, where I had withdrawn some of the money I had brought with me to Aubépine and had given instructions for the transfer of the rest of it to my bank in Dublin. So now, armed with money once again, I was about to kit myself out for life in the world. I knew exactly what I wanted. Heading for the nearest *parfumerie*, I bought a tube of Lancôme Maqui-éclat (alabaster beige); an eye-brow pencil (dark brown); a tube of lipstick (as near natural as possible) and a mirror. Feeling astonishingly better and equipped for anything, I made my way to the hairdressers.

Oh, the smell of that hairdressers, the buzz of sound, the loud

163

music! It was at the same time familiar and alien. I sat in the chair before the large mirror while the young *coiffeuse* frowned in puzzlement over my chopped and grizzled locks. I have often wondered since what she made of the strange Irishwoman who suddenly appeared in her salon with a request to put a full colour in hair that did not appear to have ever been coloured before.

'And it was so badly cut!' I imagined her telling her boyfriend that night. 'Yes, this woman was very strange! She was dressed in shabby jeans' (they were my gardening jeans – they were all I had), 'she paid in cash instead of with a credit card. Do you think perhaps she had just been released from prison?'

But if she did have any of these thoughts, she kept them to herself. She brought me a colour chart. I explained I wanted my hair to look as natural as possible. Between us we picked a colour.

'But I must warn you, you will get a great shock when you see it.' She was anxious to prepare me for the worst. 'You will not look like yourself at all!'

I didn't tell her that it was the grey-haired woman facing me in the mirror who didn't look like me at all. I had never seen myself with grey hair and I didn't like what I saw. As far as I was concerned, the transformation she was about to produce couldn't take place quickly enough.

An hour later, I looked at myself in the mirror again. Yes, there I was, more or less the old me I had been looking at for almost fifty years: a bit thinner, yes, unmade-up, certainly, but recognisably me in a way that photos of me in the Carmelite habit had never been. Something clicked back into place; in some part of my unconscious self I was beginning to get myself together again.

As my last day in Aubépine approached, it became more and more difficult to participate in any community exercise. Simply to walk into the choir for the office was liable to produce tears.

The same was true of meals in the refectory and of prayer in community – in short, any community exercise where there was sufficient silence to allow what was never far from my mind to flow in again in an unbearable surge. However, when I was occupied, I was able to banish the demons, so during those last days I lived in a frenetic whirl of physical activity. I painted the outside of window frames and window-sills all over the monastery; I scrubbed the floor of the newly decorated infirmary to within an inch of its life, so as to remove the smallest specks of paint. And of course I emptied out my cell, packed what I was going to bring with me and filled a couple of boxes with the remainder, which would be sent on to my new home in the Chemin des Oiseaux. I made phone calls to close friends to tell them about my departure, I wrote letters, I made lists of what had to be done. I only stopped when it was time for recreation, when I could listen to the inconsequential chatter of the nuns and forget for a while about the void that was always waiting to open before my feet.

And inevitably, inexorably, the last evening came. At the end of recreation, everyone said goodbye to me, as I was to leave immediately after mass in the morning, and in any event, neither Véronique nor I was anxious to have a last-minute emotional leave-taking. I had been dreading this moment, but when it came, I was dry-eyed. I seemed to have no tears left. Having said their farewells, the sisters filed out of the community room, leaving Véronique, Marie-Jeanne and me standing in an uneasy little group. After a moment's silence, Véronique proposed that we take a look at the map so that I could see the route tomorrow's journey would follow.

It would be a long journey. First I would have to take a TGV, the high-speed train, down through France as far as Lyon. There I would change to an ordinary train and travel to Valence. Finally, the last stage of my journey would bring me to St-Marcellin, from where I was to get a taxi to the Abbey of Chambarand.

As we plotted out the route and I checked my train tickets for the umpteenth time, a small frisson of excitement flickered through me. It was a faint holiday feeling, a shadow of the thrill I always felt at the beginning of a journey to a new place. It made me feel, just for an instant, that there was still happiness somewhere, and that I might be able to find it again.

While the community was at the night office, I went out for a last walk around the garden of the monastery, passing through the glass door that had seen my frantic comings and goings on the Day of the Old Beds. I made my way down Angèle's steps to Kerith, where the sweet pea I had planted had long since withered. I sat for a while on the stone bench and thought of the day I had sat there with Marie-Jeanne and promised her that everything would change. That had been a new beginning, full of hope. Now everything, every dream, my whole future, was crumbling and collapsing around me in dust. I sat there until the last rays of the sun disappeared behind the tree-tops and the night-time noises of the forest began: small mysterious rustlings and scurryings, sudden strange cries, brief whirrings of wings. The bats began their nightly ballet and I stood up to leave. I would never see Kerith again; even if I came back to visit in the future, I wouldn't be permitted to come inside the enclosure. Something was passing that I would never again be able to recapture. The finality was like that of death.

I wandered on through the deepening dusk, loath to end this farewell pilgrimage. Down towards the woods I went, right down to the place where the blackberry brambles separated the community property from the fields of a neighbouring farmer. I looked across to the far horizon, where the misty outline of the Juras could faintly be seen. From that vantage point, one could sometimes, if one was lucky, see Mont Blanc. I remembered how, as I was getting dressed early one summer morning, I had heard running feet in the corridor followed by a low tapping at my door. Alarmed, I had opened to find Angèle hopping from one foot to the other, her usually pale face flushed with excitement.

'Quick!' she had hissed. 'If you hurry, you'll see Mont Blanc!'

Half-dressed, I had rushed after her down the stairs and out into the dawn garden, where the grass was wet with dew. On down through Kerith we had gone until we had reached the blackberry bushes. And then my heart stood still, for there, where only the Juras had been before, Mont Blanc rose, towering above them like a queen, golden and white-tipped in the first rays of the morning sun. And even as we stood there, breathless and silent, she had disappeared like a dream.

And now I stood there again and recalled that brief moment of perfect happiness. Turning, I followed the track through the woods until it mounted again towards the other end of the garden. As, panting a little, I took the final steps of the steep ascent, I saw that the harvest moon had risen. Huge and golden it sat in the blackening sky, as it had sat for millions of years. It watched over Aubépine as it did over the Abbey of Chambarand where I would be tomorrow night; as it did over the as yet unimaginable Chemin des Oiseaux in Metz; as it did over the Rue de Bourgogne and the European Court of Justice in Luxembourg and the Four Courts in Dublin. In the face of that immensity and the even greater immensity of its Creator, everything was for a moment reduced to its true perspective in place and in time, and I knew that all that I was now feeling would one day pass.

Chapter 34

But the next morning I felt only loss. My train was leaving at 10 o'clock, so the plan had been that I would attend the community mass at eight, slip out at the end and have a quick breakfast, then change into civilian clothes and meet Véronique and Marie-Jeanne at the garage behind the house. They were going to drive me into town. But when I got out of bed, I knew I wouldn't be able to get through the mass without breaking down. My moral strength was at an all-time low, and the very act of putting on the habit – worse still, of taking it off – for the last time was more than I could bear. I wrote a brief note to Veronique to tell her that I wouldn't be at mass, then, dressing myself in the clothes I was to wear for the journey, I crept down the stairs and went by a roundabout route to the small community oratory, where I spent the time of morning office and mass. I didn't believe God would blame me in any way for this; I knew he understood.

Before the sisters left the chapel, I went to the refectory and had a quick cup of coffee and some bread. While I was there, Claudine came in, her pleasant face unhappy. I knew how sorry she was that it had all ended like this. She had a large packet in her hands.

'Put this in your bag in case you get hungry on the train,' she urged. I gave her a quick, grateful hug and left the refectory to collect my luggage from upstairs. As I passed the door of the little office that separated the *hôtellerie* from the nuns' part of the monastery, Annette came out.

'Ah!' she said, with an attempt at a smile, 'la grande fidèle!

You'll always be our *grande fidèle*, won't you? You won't forget us? You'll come back to see us?'

Promising her that I would, I hurried on, hoping I wouldn't meet any more members of the community. My self-control was a very fragile thing at that moment.

Véronique and Marie-Jeanne were already waiting when I made my way through the garden to the garage. Véronique was brisk and businesslike; obviously anxious to avoid any last-minute exhibitions of Celtic emotion.

'Well, here you are!' she said. 'You're lucky with the weather; it will be a perfect day for travelling.'

She was right. It was bright and sunny, but a little cooler than of late. I hesitated for a moment before getting into the car and looked for the last time at the garden.

'Come on, hop in!' Véronique said, a little impatiently. 'You don't want to miss your train!'

It occurred to me that she wanted this to be over. She wanted to see me off on that train, so that she could return and take up her community life again as though the mistake that was me had never happened. Bitterness began to rise in my throat like bile. What had I been thinking of, telling Annette that I'd come back to visit them? They wouldn't want to see me again, it would only remind them of the error of judgement they had made in accepting me in the first place. I bent to climb into the car and only then did I see Marie-Jeanne's face for the first time, as she turned towards me from the driver's seat. Her eyes were full of tears.

At the railway station, all was noise and bustle. It held almost as many memories for me as the monastery itself. The last time I had been there was the January day I had arrived to enter the Carmel, a year and a half earlier. The electronic noticeboard announced that the 10 o'clock TGV to Nice, via Lyon, was leaving from platform J in 15 minutes. We went down to platform level on the escalator. Turning to the nuns, I was about to suggest that we go and have a last cup of coffee together, when to my astonishment, Veronique suddenly gripped my shoulders, embraced me briskly and said, 'Well, this is where we leave you. Have a safe journey. We'll telephone the Abbey tonight to make sure that you've arrived safely.'

Taken aback, I turned to Marie-Jeanne and hugged her bewilderedly. They weren't even going to wait until the train came. It was all going to end just like this, on the grey platform of the crowded railway station.

Of course, later – much later – I realised the strain Véronique and Marie-Jeanne had been under that morning. Especially Marie-Jeanne, who had already, though I did not know it, begun to question her own judgement in insisting to Véronique that I should leave. But now, the fact that they were not going to wait to see me off on the train seemed the final rejection, and a door in my heart shut itself against them. It would not open again until, four months later, an Irish Jesuit priest helped me to make sense of the whole adventure and to see how essential a part of the journey and of the quest it had been.

The great TGV was pulling in to the station. 'Le TGV provenance de Paris, destination de Nice, entre en gare voie J,' cried the public address system. I picked up my case and joined the sudden rush along the platform to the carriage where my place had been reserved. I stowed my luggage and sat down. Through the window, I could see the familiar platform and, beyond it, the roofs of the old town. I was not saying goodbye to it for ever; in two weeks' time I would have to change trains here again on my way to Metz. But I would not be the same person in two weeks – indeed that person was unimaginable to me at this moment. The person I now was had just left a monastery; the person I would then be would already have spent two weeks back in the world (if the Abbey of Chambarand could be called the world!) and would presumably have moved on. That person would be on her

'God only knows ...'

way to where she lived (I couldn't think of it as 'her home') in the Chemin des Oiseaux in Metz. I didn't know that person; doubtless she would see the railway station with different eyes.

Chapter 35

I don't remember much about the journey, locked as I was inside a small world of misery. I just wanted to get to the end of it and to try to pick up the threads of life again in Chambarand. I was glad I was going there; the shock of leaving Aubépine would not be quite so brutal when cushioned by a couple of weeks in a not dissimilar environment. At Lyon, I couldn't find the platform where I had to get the train to Valence and had to rush madly to the correct one at the last minute, catching the train by the skin of my teeth. We went via Grenoble, and reached Valence about mid-afternoon. I had an hour to spare before the train to St-Marcellin was due to leave, so, in an effort to do something normal and to feel that I was once again in control of my own life and could do as I pleased, I went to the tiny café on the platform and ordered a croque-monsieur and a glass of wine. But when they arrived I couldn't finish either one. The café was full of well-dressed old ladies on their way to take the thermal baths at Val-les-Bains and, suddenly conscious of my shabby appearance (I was wearing the gardening jeans again), I made up my mind to go on a shopping expedition at the first possible opportunity.

The journey to St-Marcellin brought me north-east from Valence along a small branch line. The scenery was peaceful and green, and now that I was on the last lap of the journey, I began to relax. I would have no further trains to catch; all I had to do at St-Marcellin was to get a taxi. Véronique, who knew the place well, had assured me that I would see the taxi rank as soon as I came out of the station.

But there were no taxis waiting at the sleepy little station in St-Marcellin. I was the only passenger to get off the train. It pulled out quickly, leaving me standing on the empty platform. The ticket office was closed. Picking up my bags, I went out onto the street, but no taxis were to be seen there either. Puzzled, and somewhat alarmed, I was making my way back inside again when suddenly an ambulance came speeding urgently into the station parking lot. The driver's door swung open and a young woman jumped out and looked around. Seeing me, she ran across.

'Are you the lady for Chambarand?' she enquired.

I looked at her in disbelief. They had sent an ambulance! What on earth had Véronique told them? Did they think I was in a state of collapse?

'Well, yes,' I said, 'I'm going to Chambarand, but I think there must be some mistake ...' My voice trailed off.

Seeing my expression, the woman laughed.

'I hope you don't mind travelling in an ambulance,' she said. 'I run the taxi-cum-ambulance service here in St-Marcellin, and the same vehicle doubles for both!'

Today, the vehicle was wearing its taxi hat. Wondering what would happen if the ambulance was called out while I was travelling in the taxi, I climbed in beside her and we set off. The road wound uphill all the way, through increasingly forested terrain. The young woman, whose name was Nicole, chatted away, telling me a little about the Abbey. There was a large community there, she said, about fifty nuns. They had a huge guesthouse, which was almost always full. After a drive of about fifteen minutes, we reached tall gates concealed by a bend in the roadway. We passed under an imposing stone archway, and suddenly there before us was the Abbey.

L'Abbaye de Notre Dame du Sacré Coeur de Chambarand was a huge pile of buildings, as different from the simple little monastery in Aubépine as could be imagined. Nicole, who seemed to know her way around, drove up to a small door in one of the buildings and rang the bell. I clambered out a little stiffly as the door was opened by an elderly, rather sprightly nun dressed in cream and black.

'Hallo,' she said in English, with an unmistakeably British accent. 'I'm Sister Gloria. Welcome to Chambarand!'

A new phase of my quest had begun.

Epilogue

The leaving of Aubépine was one of the major events of my life and of the quest, and the first three months after my departure were spent in a futile struggle to come to terms with it. When the fortnight in Chambarand was over, I went to the apartment the nuns had found for me in Metz, but I couldn't settle down. After only three days, I went back to Luxembourg. There I booked into the Hotel Schintgen, a small establishment on the Rue Notre Dame, facing the cathedral. And it was in Luxembourg, while the wild ringing of the cathedral bells filled the air, that I stood one day in the Place d'Armes and read in a copy of the *Irish Times* an advertisement which said that the Irish Competition Authority was looking for a legal adviser. I applied, got the job, and came back to Ireland in October of that same year.

In Dublin, I rented a small apartment in Sydenham Road in Ballsbridge. Spiritually, I was struggling. I couldn't seem to pray any longer, and felt as though I was wandering in an inner landscape where I didn't recognise anything. I tried not to think about Aubépine. Then I met a Jesuit priest who suggested that I make a directed retreat, a thing I had never done in my life. (For those who may not know, a directed retreat is a peculiarly Jesuit thing: the retreatant spends most of the day alone in prayer and meditation, except for a brief interview with a 'director' (who might be a priest, a nun or a lay person) who listens to the retreatant's experiences of the previous twenty-four hours and helps him or her to discern what God might be saying.)

So, in January 1998, I went to Manresa House in Dollymount,

a Jesuit retreat house beautifully situated in the north of Dublin, overlooking the sea and Bull Island, and there I set about trying to make sense of my situation. On the second day, having listened to my halting and tearful attempt to explain where I was in relation to God, the community at Aubépine and myself, my director looked at me.

'You haven't grieved properly for what you've lost,' he said. 'Why don't you just stay in your room today, sit before God and let yourself feel whatever comes. You'll probably cry buckets, but that's all right!'

I blew my nose and laughed, but followed his advice, and the effect was extraordinary. I cried for hours, but as the day passed I felt a great load shift from my heart. Like a slow dawn came the realisation that there was a deep truth hidden in the experience of having apparently lost everything. That truth was that I was free. I had no plans of my own any longer. The quest could now continue without interference from me. Some lines from Francis Thompson's poem, *The Hound of Heaven*, came to me:

> Naked I wait thy Love's uplifted stroke!
> My harness piece by piece Thou hast hewn from me,
> And smitten me to my knee;
> I am defenceless utterly.
> I slept, methinks, and woke,
>   And, slowly gazing, find me stripped in sleep.

The next day, my director said to me, 'Now you must learn to trust your prayer. It may seem messy and distracted, and indeed may not seem to be prayer at all, but believe me, it is good. Trust it, go with it. After all, when you pray, you are not the only person involved. Do you think God does nothing during prayer? Trust him now; let go, and see what he will do.'

Over the next weeks and months, I followed his advice, and began to relax into a way of prayer that, although it was wordless and brought none of the feelings of peace I remembered from the past, yet fed my inner hunger in some way that I didn't understand. Together with this, my initial realisation of a hidden truth deepened and rooted itself in me, so that by the time I paid my first visit to Aubépine in March of that year, I was able to tell Véronique and Marie-Jeanne that I knew they had been right. More than that, I knew that the experience of losing everything had been so essential to the quest I was still engaged in that I now saw it as the purpose of my entering Aubépine in the first place. In other words, leaving was the whole point of going there. 'He who would save his life must lose it ...' the Gospel tells us, and for the first time I understood what it meant.

From that point, my life changed. The more I lived out of the truth of that experience, the more I realised that it is absolutely essential that a moment should come in the spiritual quest where all your resources, all your plans and hopes and dreams, are taken away. That is a moment of crisis. You can then do one of two things: abandon the quest as being hopeless, or turn to God in the most absolute way, and allow him to 'be God'. If you take that second option, God is at last free to act in your life as he wants, and your life will become directed along his path. In St John of the Cross's poem *Dark Night* there is a verse which describes how the person undertaking the quest sets out without any light 'save that which burned in my heart'. That, St John explains, is the light of faith, and of course only by faith can we ever know God in this life. And so he continues:

> That light guided me
> More surely than the light of noonday
> To the place where he (well I knew who!)
> Awaited me
> A place where none appeared.

That was how the inner landscape of my life developed after Aubépine. Externally, of course, there were also difficulties. I hadn't practised law for two years; indeed, I hadn't even thought about it during that time. Now I found that my confidence was shaken, and although I had been lucky enough to get a job very quickly, I felt very unsure of myself. However, my employers seemed happy enough, my colleagues were warmly welcoming and, little by little, my confidence increased. After some time, I moved from Ballsbridge to a larger apartment overlooking the sea near Sutton. Like the apartment where the whole story had begun, it had a balcony, but while the first balcony looked out on woods and hills, this one overlooked the sea and Howth Head. On summer evenings I sat there as the light faded, and watched the ferry from Holyhead as it crawled into Dublin Bay like a huge illuminated caterpillar. I prayed often on that balcony, but I sat there too with friends, and we drank wine as the sun sank on the horizon, burning a path into the waters of the Irish Sea. And the prayer was good, and the friendship was good, and it was very good to be home again.

And then, some two years after my departure from Aubépine, I was appointed as one of four High Court Inspectors to investigate the Ansbacher affair, a tax fraud involving offshore accounts in the Cayman Islands, that had been uncovered in the course of a tribunal of enquiry known as the McCracken Tribunal, set up to enquire into the making of certain payments to politicians.

Ironically, I must at that time have been one of the few people in Ireland who hadn't heard of the Ansbacher scandal. The dogs in the street knew about Ansbacher, but it meant nothing to me that June evening in 1999, when, just as I was about to leave the office for home, I took a telephone call from the Secretary General of the Department of Enterprise, Trade and Employment, asking me if I would be willing to accept the appointment. The McCracken Tribunal and all that had flowed from it had taken place in my absence and I knew nothing of it.

A hectic period then began. The investigation lasted three years, and my life during that time could not have been more different from the secluded life I had led in Aubépine. Together with my three fellow Inspectors, the then Circuit Court Judge Sean O'Leary (now a judge of the High Court), Paul Rowan FCA, a retired partner of Pricewaterhouse Coopers, and Michael Cush, Senior Counsel, I found myself to some extent in the public gaze, as the investigation was the subject of considerable media attention. I travelled to the Cayman Islands, where documents crucial to the investigation were retained. And yet, in the midst of all the activity and all the external changes in my life (I bought a house too during this period), I was discovering more and more that the quest for God does not require seclusion in a monastery. The new way of praying that I had learned from my Jesuit director was leading me to places that were deeper and stranger than any I had experienced in Aubépine. This inner journey was in some strange way knitting itself to the outer one, so that increasingly I was possessed by a sense of everything in my life becoming simplified and unified. And in this unification, Aubépine found its rightful place.

For although Aubépine is part of my past, it is part too of my present. It has contributed to the making and shaping of me. It opened doors in my mind through which I caught glimpses of my hidden self. Those glimpses led me to deeper examinations of the dark side of my own nature and to acceptance of it. Aubépine was a catalyst, but even more, it was the bridge over the troubled waters of my search for God. Once I had crossed that bridge, I discovered that I had taken a giant step forward on the journey.

The nuns of Aubépine have remained my friends. The little red and cream *hôtellerie* is my oasis in the desert, the place to which I go whenever the living water in the well sinks low. Véronique and Marie-Jeanne are still there, happy always to see me, but even happier that I have understood why they had to let me go. I discuss it more with Marie-Jeanne than I do with Véronique, because I know that she needs more reassurance about my affection for her, about the peace that I have found in my life, about the fact that the whole adventure had to turn out as it did.

Angèle, my old companion of the novitiate, is still there too, now finally professed and a fully fledged member of the community. Sometimes now it is she who opens the door of the *hôtellerie* to me when I arrive for a visit, because my dear Annette has gone, she who was so sad when her *'grande fidèle'* had to leave. One morning a few years ago, she felt unwell. The doctor was called and proposed a few tests in the hospital. Yvette, Marie-Jeanne's friend, drove her to the same hospital that I had gone to the night I broke my Achilles tendon. But Annette never came home again. She faded quietly and, three days after she left her beloved Aubépine, she died. The *hôtellerie* is not the same without her. 'Ah, voici la grande fidèle!' Claudine says now, whenever I go there, and I know that we are both remembering Annette.

But life goes on and the community has changed considerably in the seven years that have passed since my departure. Four others besides Annette have died – including Marie-Cécile, at whose jubilee I was dancing when I broke the tendon. And five new members have joined, so that when I look at the community now from my place in the chapel, it looks very different from the community I gazed at, appalled, on the evening of my first visit. The age profile has changed too and now six of the eighteen nuns are between the ages of twenty-two and forty-two, an extraordinary statistic in today's terms.

And my bête noir, the enclosure fence, has been completed. The last time I was at Aubépine, I traced from the outside its descent to the Prairie, and remembered, and thought how greatly my life had changed, and thanked the God for whom I continue to search, who, paradoxically, shows me the way I must follow.

> In solitude she lived and in solitude now has built her nest
> And in solitude her dear one alone guides her, who
> likewise in solitude was wounded by love.
>
> (St John of the Cross, *The Spiritual Canticle*)